Still TAKING THE LAND

LESSONS FROM FOUR DECADES OF CHURCH PLANTING

WITH
WAYMAN MITCHELL
AND
GREG MITCHELL

EDITED BY DAVID J. DRUM

FOREWORD BY HAROLD S. WARNER

KIDWELL
PUBLISHING

Published by Kidwell Publishing
www.kidwellpublishing.com
ISBN: 978-0-9817634-9-1
Printed in the United States of America
ALL RIGHTS RESERVED

Table of Contents

Foreword by Harold S. Warner

I was thinking about a *New Year's theme*: not a gimmick or a catch phrase but a *word in season*, something that the Lord was saying to our church for this year. I can remember it clearly; I was in the prayer room in San Jose, CA when a *distinct* word came to me, **Increase!** I immediately started writing notes (the famous HSW scribble) about where increase stood out in Scripture. The realization that came to me was that increase was so much more than just money, numbers or things. What stood out was not the *year of increase*, which could be presumptuous (we set the date, or time frame), but *The God of Increase*. This is who God is at any time, season, or circumstance. He is the God of increase! That is a wonderful explanation for what has taken place in our fellowship over the last four decades.

The word increase is the Greek word *auzano* which means to *grow, increase,* or *enlarge*. It speaks to the **growth of that which lives** naturally or spiritually. The problem is that to some degree the word has been hijacked by a false prosperity Gospel and false expectations or definitions of ministry success (*noise, numbers and nickels*). What is needed and called for is a *Biblical theology* of increase: having our hearts and worlds *framed by the Word of God*. The Bible talks about the increase of the *Word of God* (Acts 12:24); the increase of *disciples* (Acts 6:7); the increase of *love* (1Thess.3:12); the increase of *strength* (Isa.40:29); the increase of *revelation*; and the increase of *faith* (2Cor.10:15).

One evangelist observed, "Here is the frustration of every pastor I preach for. It has to do with growth. I have spent time with pastors all year long that are baffled by lack of growth. I have emphasized over and over again how the bottom line is: it is God that brings the increase and they need personally to lay hold of God for that increase. It is His church that He is building through them." That is why I am not particularly fond of the term *church growth* and will not be writing my book on it anytime soon! A more realistic term would be *church seasons.* Leslie Newbigin struck the right balance, I believe, in his book *The Open Secret.* He wrote, "Reviewing the teaching of the New Testament, one would have to say, on the one hand, there is joy in the rapid growth of the church in the earliest days, but on the other, there is no evidence that numerical growth of the church is a matter of primary concern. There is no shred of evidence in Paul's letters to suggest that he judged the churches by the measure of their success in rapid numerical growth. [Nowhere is there] anxiety or an enthusiasm about the numerical growth of the church." I have a better approach: ***church health and witness***; things that can be done no matter what the season might be. A wise pastor once said, "You take care of the depth of your ministry; let God take care of the breadth."

Let me give you three things to ponder that capture the essence of a vision for *The God of Increase.*

The Reasonable Expectation

This expectation is reasonable because God has built this dynamic into creation, and because it is based on the nature of His kingdom. *"Of the increase of his government and peace there shall be no end* (Isaiah 9:7a KJV)." His kingdom is an increasing kingdom! This is why in the Parable of the Talents, the master's reasonable expectation was the increase of the goods he had entrusted to his servants (Matthew 25:27). When talking about the life of faith Peter said, *"For if these qualities are yours and are increasing, they keep you from being ineffective or unfruitful in the knowledge of our Lord Jesus Christ* (2 Peter 1:8 ESV)." Real increase tends toward a God-inspired and a Word-framed vision for our lives, our walk with God, our relationships, our finances, and our Church. I have a friend who because of unique circumstances has found himself being a temporary *church shopper*. What stood out to him was <u>how little vision</u> there is in so many churches!? It is all about people feeling good, comfortable, entertained, and there is very little doctrinal content.

The Divine Dimension

Paul said in his classic description of ministry, *"I have planted, Apollos watered; but God gave the increase* (1 Corinthians 3:6 KJV)." Our hope and confidence is in the God who gives the increase. Again, true vision does not settle into a selfish agenda, where it is all about me; instead, it puts the focus where it needs to be, on God, His person, power, and kingdom! Paul goes on to say, *"So then neither he who plants is anything, nor he who waters, but God who gives the increase* (1 Corinthians 3:7 NKJV)." The Message Translation says, *"It's not the one who plants or the one who waters who is at the **center** of this process but God, who makes things grow."* What we are contending for in our lives, churches, and fellowship is the reality of a divine dimension.

The Revolutionary Call

I was reading where one pastor was asking another, "What did you do to get people to come?" He was expecting to hear how he initiated several programs, sent out mass mailings, instituted a demographic study of his city, fed the hungry, and taught about *40 Days On Purpose*. The pastor said, "I didn't do anything but be faithful. God built the church through people talking to people and getting excited about Jesus and their church." Hmmm, what a novel concept! People excited about Jesus with a vision and a will to work for the Lord! This call and process is embodied in some of John the Baptist's last words. As Jesus' earthly ministry was growing, John's was coming to an end, and he was asked how he felt about that. He responded, *"He must increase, but I must decrease* (John 3:30)." This call has never been rescinded, and is still in effect today. It still represents our marching orders!

We all marvel at what God has done in our fellowship! Looking forward we have a fantastic promise to hold on to. It is the promise of **more** in all the areas that really matter. *"Every detail works to your advantage and to God's glory: more and more grace, more and more people, more and more praise* (2 Corinthians 4:15 MSG)!" This book contains principles that have been our guide, the vision that has been our passion, and the miracle that comes from the *God of Increase.*

Harold S. Warner

The Heavenly Vision
by Greg Mitchell

Therefore, King Agrippa, I was not disobedient to the heavenly vision... Acts 26:19 NKJV

Paul the Apostle was brought before King Agrippa to answer charges brought against him. Paul at this time is very close to the end of his life and in order to explain where he is today and where he is supposed to go until he dies, he tells the story of where he came from. He says, "There was a vision." This was a heavenly vision or blue print that required Paul's obedience. In other words, everything he was doing lined up with the vision that God revealed.

During a building project at church the construction crew was using a GPS device to do the surveying with pinpoint satellite accuracy. I inquired how surveying was done in the old days before GPS. His answer was, in simple terms, you needed to have fixed points to line up with. If you had high reference points you could see, then you could tell where you were and line up with that. If there were no high points they would have to be erected somehow, otherwise there was nothing to line up with.

When I was a missionary in South Africa I got talking with a young man who said he was a Christian from a church called Apostolic Faith Mission. I had read about the revival that birthed these churches and the founder John G. Lake, so I commented about the powerful history of his fellowship. He looked at me very puzzled, obviously having never heard this before. I elaborated for a few moments about John G. Lake in the early part of the century being used by God to plant so many churches, now numbering in the thousands throughout Africa. This young man then got this very spiritual look on his face and said, "We are not into the past, we are only into what God is doing now and in the future."

The problem with that is this: You need reference points. If you do not know where you came from then you will not have anything to line up with to tell you where you are going.

I want to tell the story of our fellowship and the vision we have. How did we get here? Where did the vision come from? This will give us reference points so we know where we are. It is very important for us to understand so we know the road ahead.

Preparation for Vision

The vision of our fellowship came through my father, Pastor Wayman Mitchell. First, I want you to understand very clearly that my parents were not church going people. My father had never attended church his entire life and my mother had only a few times as a child. They were sinners who liked to smoke, drink, dance, and fight...and that was just my mom! (When I first made that joke during a sermon my mom told me afterwards it was not far from the truth). They were living in Phoenix, Arizona and at the young age of twenty-five they had a crisis in their lives. Their first born child Terry, my oldest sister, died suddenly when she was ten months old of pneumonia. You can imagine the desperation and confusion they were feeling. It was during this critical moment in their lives that my uncle George and my aunt Ione witnessed to my parents. They went to church with them and got powerfully converted and experienced a dramatic life change. On the morning my dad was filled with the Holy Ghost he began to speak in tongues loudly and prophesy. This went on and on for more than an hour. Finally, everybody in the church left and they told my mom to lock up whenever he finished.

From the very beginning of his salvation there was a desire to do something for God. He began to witness. They did not have many organized outreaches like we have, this was something birthed in his heart. He began to go with a few people down to the local parks of Glendale to witness and testify. He wanted other people to have what he had and to know the wonderful things that Jesus had done for him.

The desire to pray was also in his heart. In our fellowship we are used to having prayer each morning and having prayer before each church service. The church my parents were saved in only had prayer meetings once a week and that was for a few minutes on a Wednesday night. My father wanted God to use his life; he wanted to see other people saved. Even though Phoenix is around one-hundred degrees half the year he would pray and cry out to God every morning in a little tin shed in the back of his house.

In wanting to be used by God he went to his pastor for direction. There was no discipleship or church planting, the only answer they had was Bible College. So, he packed up the family and moved to Los Angeles, California to attend Life Bible College. It was not at all what he expected. For one thing, many of the students he went to college with were not even saved! They were getting in trouble so their parents sent them to Bible College in the hopes that it would do some good. So because of this powerful conversion, he is working and supporting his family while attending school so he can do something for God and a lot of the students are anything but serious about the ministry. The other discouraging dynamic was the unbelief of the professors. They were teaching the Bible and yet did not believe what it said. They did not believe in the rapture, in speaking in tongues, or in healing. He spent most of his years at Bible College arguing with his professors that the Bible was true. It also began to dawn on my dad that none of his professors were successful pastors. The reason they were teaching was because they had never been able to build a church. They were trying to teach people how to do something they were unable to do themselves. All this caused my dad to be disillusioned with the whole concept of Bible College.

He did graduate however, and became a pastor in the Foursquare denomination. When he began his ministry they only gave him very small churches with very big problems. But he threw himself into it with all his heart. Programs for kids were the method for building churches and reaching the world taught to him in school. They take this from a scripture in Isaiah that says, *"and a little child shall lead them* (Isaiah 11:6 NKJV)." The theory was if you will do programs and get a lot of kiddies to come, then they will get their parents to come and you will be able to reach the whole world. And so my dad threw himself into Sunday School programs for kids. He did everything that they had taught him; gimmicks like giving away giant chocolate bars and allowing the kids to break LP records over his head if they set an attendance record. Kids did come, however he quickly became disenchanted with this approach, because he had been powerfully converted from sin and that is what he wanted to see. It dawned on him that what he was doing was not working. If he got the kids to come it did not mean the father would come. He knew instinctively that if the dad would get saved he would bring the wife and kids to church. But it was not happening with the methods he had been taught. Over time, he became extremely discouraged.

So, he quit! Through a series of events and several church assignments he grew tired of the denominational politics and the programs that were not bringing conversions as he had experienced and wanted to see in others. He called up his area supervisor and said, "I QUIT! I'm finished, I've already turned in the keys and I'm not going back. It's over, I'm leaving the ministry." The supervisor responded, "Well, before you quit, there is a church that has opened up in your hometown of Prescott, Arizona. Maybe you would be interested in going to look at it because you are from the area." Once again, it was a church with great problems: The pastor and his son were both committing adultery and had run off with women from the church. Most of the congregation had moved on, all that was left was a handful of people. For some reason, my dad agreed to consider this last assignment.

He and my mother discussed it during the trip. They knew that in this little group of people there were two couples in their late twenties, almost thirty. Most of the others were elderly. My parents agreed that if these two younger couples would commit to staying in the church then they would take the pastorate. If not, they would quit the ministry altogether. That was their agreement. They came into Prescott Valley and went to the restaurant where these two ladies (the wives of the young couples) were working. They introduced themselves and told them they were thinking of coming there to pastor the church. My dad told them our family would come if they agreed to stay in the church. After discussing it they said, "Ok, if you come we will stay, we promise to stay." One of those ladies is Sharon Allen who plays the organ in the church to this day, and her husband Bob – our head usher and church pilot. So, in January of 1970 we moved to Prescott, Arizona and Pastor Mitchell became the pastor of the church.

Revealing the Vision

Evangelism

Evangelism is a foundational principle of who we are as a fellowship. Using music as a tool to reach souls evolved from humble beginnings. Two young couples had gotten saved and started attending the church. As my dad began sharing his burden for souls they told him of the tremendous interest that young people had in music, and explained that a concert would draw them to church. It was a great idea, but of course you need a band and a PA system to put on a concert and the church had neither. These two young people said they could play a little guitar and they had a dope smoking friend that would be willing to play, so that was the band for the first concert. My dad rented the old Boys Club hall and a PA system that would be equivalent to a home stereo today. He printed up some hand drawn flyers announcing the big event which they passed out around town. That night they had over 250 people with about 50 answering an altar call for salvation. When I shared this recently in the Prescott church, a lady told me how she was converted in that first concert and is still in the church all these years later.

It became clear through events like this that our call is to take the gospel beyond the four walls of the church, rather than sitting in the church building and hoping that sinners somehow will come. My dad heard of what God was doing in what we now call the Jesus Movement. He took some young men with him and went to California to Huntington Beach. It was there he saw a man named Larry Reed who was boldly preaching on the beach and declaring the gospel. After seeing that and attending a few 'coffee-house' concert ministries, he knew this is what he wanted. He knew they needed to confront sinners where they were. So my dad invited Larry Reed to bring what he was doing to Prescott and they set a date. He thought that Larry was going to bring a massive team with a huge band, but when he showed up it was only him and two recently converted heroin addict girls who played acoustic guitar. However, during that weekend for the first time, people in the church went to the downtown plaza and boldly preached and declared on the streets Jesus Christ. At the local County Fair they stood up on tables and preached the gospel and four people got arrested. This made the newspapers and caused quite a stir. The rumor began to go around that at the church they were passing out drugs in the offering plate. The next service the building was packed! The young people had to see this.

Pastor Mitchell came to the understanding that our call is to create a platform to declare the Gospel; you either find a crowd or create a crowd so that you can declare the gospel. They started the weekly concert ministry. For years it was every Friday and Saturday nights and the young people would pack the place. They showed movies. Back in 1970 there were only two Christian movies to choose from, but they showed them over and over again because that was creating a crowd. They would also go find a crowd at a football game or out on the plaza downtown. Wherever people gather was considered a place to declare the gospel.

From the early days of this revival came the desire to expand our reach. Pastor Mitchell wanted other people to have what he was experiencing in Prescott. Ministries in surrounding towns were hearing about the move of God among young people, and would ask for help to see that happen in their communities. This is where impact teams were birthed. The church folks would load up in cars and travel to Phoenix, Cottonwood, or other neighboring towns to bring the gospel of Jesus Christ. Our call is evangelism. Every believer is called to be a witness. This is a foundational part of our vision as a fellowship.

The Power of the Local Church

Many Christians do not believe that a local church is enough. One way this expresses itself is in the belief that in order to reach our city we have to get all of the churches to join together and then we become powerful. A single local church is insufficient. The Para-church movement also comes from this belief that the local church is lacking. These are groups that spring up to help the church function in special areas like worship, evangelism, or especially the training of workers. Most of the church world functions this way.

Many of the young men that were getting saved began to catch a vision of being used by God. Several came to Pastor Mitchell to get direction and he gave them the only option that he knew, which was going to Bible school. He sent two young men off so that they could be trained to be men of God, but both of them lost the fire and started to believe strange things. It had ruined them. My dad knew there had to be another way. God began to show him the plan for reaching the world is through the local church. In other words, everything that God is going to do on the earth is going to come through a local congregation. If that is missions, training workers, whatever it might be, it is within and through the local church.

> God has put everything under his feet and has made him the head of everything for the good of the church, which is his body, <u>the fullness of the one who fills everything in every way</u>. Ephesians 1:22-23 ISV

At first he did not understand all of the ramifications of this vision, but as time went by he saw that God was restoring the understanding and dignity of the local church. In time he would see that this would encompass many areas; from the training of men to how we fulfill the great commission.

Discipleship

How did Jesus train men? The Jews had many rabbinical schools for learning scriptures. But, he did not send men to school. The method Jesus used was hands-on instruction. This is 1) impartation of his spirit and vision. 2) It was to see a godly example and how he functioned day to day and in different circumstances. 3) He involved the disciples in on-the-job training.

This was Pastor Mitchell's approach from the early days. He was not exactly hip with the young people that God was bringing. You have to picture in your mind my dad wearing white shoes with lime green pants. He did not try to be cool with the hippies but instead he trained young men how to run the concert, how to preach, and outreach. They either made it work or fell flat on their face. The emphasis was on character development and catching the spirit of revival that was in the heart of their pastor. In the Bible school all you must do is pass the tests. You can be beating your wife, a porno freak, and a thief, but as long as you can make a passing grade they hand you a diploma and label you a man of God. Discipleship focuses rather on what kind of man you are.

The Bible tells us the things to look for in a man of God are how he treats his wife, raises his children, how he uses money, and what is his testimony on the job (1 Timothy 3:1-13; Titus 1:6-8). The emphasis is on character, spirit, fruitfulness, and effectiveness in ministry.

Church Planting

Church planting is the natural outflow of discipleship. In the early days of sending impact teams to churches asking for help, we would do a concert in the evening after evangelizing during the day, street preaching, and passing out invitations for the event. It was not uncommon to see from fifty to over one-hundred people saved in a single day's effort. It would be a powerful impact, but then we would say goodbye and go back home. The problem was two-fold:

On the one hand, many of the people who were getting saved were not respectable church going people. They were dirty, they were smelly, and their lives were a total wreck. We would leave all these converts whom most of the churches did not want. They wanted clean-cut religious people like themselves. (In one of the early impact teams to Phoenix, a young lady from the church they were trying to help saw the strange-looking hippies brought in to the concert by evangelism and said to my dad, "Wayman, I sure hope you know what you're doing!"). So all these new converts wound up being rejected, looked down upon, and given the message they were not welcome.

On the other hand, if they were accepted, it did not take long for them to become lukewarm Christians filled with strange doctrines. This became very discouraging to the laborers, and obviously was not working. Pastor Mitchell realized that the best thing to do was have a man in these cities that had the same spirit and vision that he had. He thought, "We must have men who share our hearts for evangelism, who will love these people, who will welcome them and work with them, who will

9

believe the doctrines that we believe so that these converts will be grounded in truth." He concluded that the only way that was going to happen was if we began to train the men and plant them in these towns and cities. When he presented this to the congregation they rallied behind the plan.

The first couple raised up and trained in house to be launched was Harold and Mona Warner. It was announced that they were going into a small town called Kearny, Arizona. In this town was a group of Christians who needed a pastor and had heard about what God was doing in Prescott. Harold and another brother went to speak with these people and get a feel for the area before moving into town. That day they witnessed and preached at a parade and this basically freaked these church people out and caused them to change their mind. They decided it was not what they wanted. They felt our style of evangelism upset people and told Harold to go back home. On their way back home to Prescott to discuss this with Pastor Mitchell, tragically, they had a terrible accident. It was raining and the car slid off the road, breaking Harold's back and paralyzing him from the waist down.

You can imagine the somber mood in the Prescott church after this happened. There was an outcry among some people that this was a sign that this church planting thing was obviously not of God, and he was removing his blessing. But my dad knew a very important principle in life is once God reveals his will you do not turn your back on it simply because things do not go as planned. The next Sunday morning service Pastor Mitchell stood up and declared, "Not only are we not changing our minds about church planting, but for every one that the devil attacks like this we will send a hundred more in their place." He challenged couples to stand that day and answer the call to go and pioneer a church and many responded. So, while Harold was recovering in the hospital, they planted the first church to the metropolis of Wickenburg, Arizona. Wickenburg back then was eighteen hundred cowboys; that was the entire population. We sent a couple who did exactly what they had been taught in Prescott, and found out that it worked. People began to get saved just like in Prescott and in less than six months it was a fully self-supporting congregation. Three months after being discharged from the hospital, Harold and Mona Warner were sent to Tucson, Arizona where they are to this day.

Other couples began to be raised up. It was not Pastor Mitchell assigning men here or there, but people began to speak to him about certain cities being on their hearts and they were praying for churches to be planted in those towns. We began to expand initially close by in Arizona, and then New Mexico, but it was people who caught the vision and felt called to go to other places where they did not have revival and to reach them with the gospel. This began the vision to birth churches with workers we train to reproduce what was happening in their mother church.

World Evangelism

It's seems simple enough now that world evangelism means the whole world. However, for the church in Prescott in the mid-seventies, this was quite an enlargement of vision that did not come automatically. I remember in those days we would take family vacations to spots where my dad was thinking about planting a church. On one of those trips as a kid we went to the incredible resort spot of Nogales, Arizona. A young man from the Prescott church was living just across the Mexico border in Nogales, Sonora. He had been in the U.S. illegally and come to Prescott looking for work. Somebody witnessed to him and he got powerfully converted. He stayed as long as he could but finally it was evident he was going to have to go back to Mexico. We planted a work in Nogales, Arizona. It did not do real well; they were struggling with very few people getting saved and not a lot happening. However, when the worker would go across the border to visit the convert

11

from Prescott, a good size group would gather because he had been witnessing to his family and friends. After this went on for a while, the worker called Pastor Mitchell with the bright idea of moving the church across the border into Mexico. We cannot appreciate now what a big step this was. There were all sorts of questions and anxiety, but finally the decision was made and the church was planted in Nogales, Sonora. Almost immediately it began to explode with revival. The "Arizona Fellowship" was now international! Two nations!

The next nation was Holland. Pastor Mitchell received an invitation from somebody he knew from Bible school who was now a pastor in Holland. Through that trip he made some initial contacts and so we planted a work there. That began to thrive, just like it did in Prescott.

Then, in 1977, another friend from Bible school invited Pastor Mitchell to come preach in Australia. He spent nearly a month preaching throughout cities in Western Australia, not knowing anything about the culture. He simply declared the gospel exactly like he would in Prescott, and to his astonishment, the people responded just like they would back home.

Pastor Mitchell was coming to the conclusion that the gospel works wherever it is preached. It worked in Prescott, then Mexico, then Holland. So now Australia began to be the burden of his heart. He felt if we had churches there with men who believed like us, we could have a powerful revival in that nation. In 1978, for the first time, we stood up a couple and challenged the conference body to give financially and help launch them, not to the next State, but to the other side of the planet, into Perth, West Australia. The vision was to build up a church just like in Prescott that would train national workers to reach their own people and eventually carry on the work themselves. The work there exploded in revival and we saw that this indeed was a 'Heavenly Vision' that works all over the world!

These simple five principles are the foundation of who we are as a fellowship and crucial to maintaining the course God has given: Evangelism, the importance of the local church, discipleship, church planting, and world evangelism. This pattern still works. You can create a crowd, draw a crowd, preach the gospel, get people saved, give them a ministry expression, stir in them calling, disciple them, raise finances, and plant churches. It works all over the world; in every nation we have planted a worker.

Buying Into the Vision
What does this have to do with you, the reader? Anytime someone has a vision and they begin to share it, the crucial factor is people buying into the vision. That means if you agree with the vision then you line-up your heart and your actions to see it come to pass. I want to be bluntly honest with you; the vision described here is very expensive. To reach the world, to see genuine converts, to make disciples, and to touch the nations is very expensive. If you are looking for a church that is not going to ask much of your time, do not come to one of our churches! I can recommend numerous charismatic churches that will not ask anything of you. They do not care if you come or not because they are not trying to do what we are doing. They are having church, we are reaching the world. If you are looking for a church that will not ask much money from you, do not come to one of our churches because what we do is incredibly expensive. Typically, when we plant a worker oversees in a faraway place, by the time that we have moved them there, got them a vehicle, bought them equipment, and got them a meeting venue, we have spent about sixty-thousand dollars or so. We had a worker a few years back that in the first seven months cost one hundred and forty-four thousand dollars! What we do is expensive. It is worth it, but it is very expensive. We can't play at it, or dabble in it. It requires people who see the vision and fully commit themselves to it.

I experienced a very powerful conversion when I was a teenager. I left the major sins that I was involved in, but as far as where my life was headed, I had my own plans. I wanted God to help me with relationships, fix my problems, get me a job, and money. I never asked what he wanted, it was all about me. In 1981, when I was seventeen years old, my parents moved to Perth, West Australia to take the pastorate of the church there. It was like stepping back in time ten years. It felt like the Prescott church in the early days of the Jesus Movement. They were experiencing a powerful weekly concert scene where dozens of young people were being radically converted. After seeing this I decided to move there with them, even though I was about to graduate from high school. Not long after that, during a discipleship class, my father was teaching on how to prepare sermons. I was in the back just looking at the young men who were gathered, and God spoke to me about the heavenly vision for my life. He told me he wanted me to preach. That night on the way I home I told my father that God had spoken about the call of God for my life.

Shortly after that we had what was called a vision luncheon. Basically, after church one afternoon we ate some chicken and Pastor Mitchell spoke about the vision for Australia and that church in Perth. He simply brought a map of Australia, explained about discipleship and church planting, where we had come from and what he saw for the future. He spoke about reaching all the towns of Australia with the gospel and how some of the young men present might be the ones God was calling. He asked them to begin naming places where they would like to see churches. People started calling out names of towns they would like to see churches planted in. I had never been to any other city in Australia, except for Perth. I did not know where these places were and could not even pronounce many of them, but as they were calling out these cities something began to stir me on the inside. I thought perhaps I could go there, or there. One new convert said we should send a church to Kalgoorlie.

She said, "There are a hell of a lot of miners there, and they are all sinners and need Jesus." She was right on target. That is exactly why we need to go there. That day I caught a vision and surrendered to go wherever God wanted me.

What do you want your local church to become? Every person who attends must decide. Do you just want to have a cozy safe place for the family where you can feel sheltered from the world? You can have that. Do you just want to attend a few services a week and hear nice sermons about heaven and the blessings of God? You have to decide. Or, do you want to reach the lost and make impact in the world for Christ? Do you want your church to be a church planting center, because every church we plant should be making disciples and planting churches. You have to decide. What do you want your church to become?

What are you willing to do to see that happen? If you want to be a church planting center it is expensive. What is your part in that? Are you willing to pay the price with your time? If we are going to reach the world we cannot be like everybody else. God needs men who are excellent. If you want to be lazy you are not going to reach the world. If you want to be carnal and sinful you cannot reach the world. What is it that you are willing to do to see your church make an impact?

Stop for a moment and think about where you would like to see a new church planted. Is it a place in your area or regions beyond? Jesus is the Lord of the harvest. There is a reason why one person is drawn to a city or a nation and another is not. God puts it in the heart of his laborer. First of all begin to pray for that place. Pray to the Lord of the harvest to send laborers. Many of the churches we have now are the result of the people of God praying. I will never forget when I was probably nineteen years old, my wife and I were at a conference and we were watching a world evangelism video. God did something in my heart for Africa. While I am watching this video I began to weep and tell God we need churches in Africa. I did not even understand how that could be possible for a little white boy from Prescott, but if he needed me I was willing. I began to pray for Africa. It was not until years later that we planted our lives in South Africa, but it began in prayer. Pray for laborers, but know that God might call you to be the answer to your own prayer.

I was very young when I responded to the gospel. I was sent out from Perth, Australia to pioneer when I was twenty-one years old. I went to one of those cities mentioned in that vision luncheon. Since then I have preached all over the world, literally, and seen God do wonderful things. Through the years I have observed some of my peers who chose a different course. They pursued career or money. They can now show their nice homes with manicured lawns, new cars and a boat in the driveway. But I have no regrets. At a young age I lined up my life with the heavenly vision and there is no amount you could give me to trade that away. If I could show you some of the converts that God has given me...some of them are preaching the gospel now and planting churches... Could I trade that for a house or a boat? I would rather be reaching the world!

I am challenging you to line up your life with the heavenly vision. This gospel works. I have seen men of all colors and languages and cultures come to Christ. When they catch the vision they make impact on the world around them. You can make an impact if you would let God use your life. Pray to God right now that if he needs somebody to go you would be willing, and then follow-up that prayer with action. If you are not called to go, then tell God you will do everything in your power to make sure that other people can go, because that is our call. We have got to reach the world for Christ.

Double or Nothing
by Wayman Mitchell

I heard a story of a man who walked into a Las Vegas casino with two suitcases in his hands. In one was seven-hundred-fifty-thousand dollars in cash, and the other one was empty. He got his chips, walked up to one of the gaming tables, and in one turn of the wheel gambled it all. It was double or nothing. He won seven-hundred-fifty-thousand dollars and did what most people do not have enough sense to do; he cashed in his chips, loaded it all back in the suitcases, caught a taxi and left town. He was heard to remark, "Inflation is eating this stuff up so fast, that I figured I might as well gamble it all, double it, or lose it all anyway." That is an interesting mentality, is it not? I do not recommend it, of course. Casinos in Las Vegas put up three-million dollar signs paid for by people who have tried that. One thing we can say about this man is that he has correctly seen the signs of his times and the age in which he lives. He saw an opportunity, seized it, and gambled everything, double or nothing.

> *...it seemed good to us, being assembled with one accord, to send chosen men to you with our beloved Barnabas and Paul, men who have risked their lives for the name of our Lord Jesus Christ. We have therefore sent Judas and Silas, who will also report the same things by word of mouth. Acts 15:25-26 NKJV*

The Call of God

History has many illustrations of men who took risks. One is the story of Pizarro, a Panamanian-Spanish explorer who, with his crew of conquerors, had filled ten long years with the hardships of his first two expeditions. The heat of the deserts, the stinking swamps and jungles, followed by the bitter cold of mountain peaks and constant attacks of savage Indians, had worn the life out of every one of his men. They were brought to a point of decision. Two ships were waiting to take them back to Panama. Pizarro took his sword and drew a line from the east to the west with great determination. After he had looked at these men, he pointed south where they had suffered such misery, heartache, death, and destitution. He said, "Friends and comrades, this is the side of death, hardship, hunger, nakedness, bones, and abandonment. The other side is that of pleasure. To the north you may go to be poor, to the south to Peru to be rich. Let every good Spaniard choose which suits him best." One hundred and eighty-three brave men crossed the line. A boat turned immediately towards Panama with the quitters, and Pizarro and his men turned the other ship to Peru, and changed the course of history.

You have heard of Cortez and the story of when he landed at Vera Cruz, Mexico in 1615, and began his dramatic conquest of Mexico. He had seven-hundred men under his command. He purposely set fire to the eleven ships that had brought them from Spain, pushed them out into the Gulf of Mexico, and watched as they stood on shore the only means of retreat burn. When the last ember sank beneath the waves, they turned and marched into the depths of Mexico prepared for whatever they might meet. Cortez also changed the course of history.

In 1969, the world just simply went ape over the men who landed on the moon. It was a tremendous accomplishment when Neil Armstrong became the first man who ever set foot upon the moon. Can you imagine those men sitting on that capsule at Cape Canaveral, Florida, during the countdown? No one had ever done what they were going to do; no one had ever walked on the moon. Things went through their minds, just like what goes through the minds of anybody facing the unknown, but they were brave men and willing to roll the dice.

The Gospel calls us to risk. We find in this passage of scripture a tremendous statement made concerning Paul and Barnabas. They were *men who have risked their lives (Acts 15:26 NKJV)."* Literally, this means they surrendered, exposed, and endangered their lives. They gambled their lives for the name of the Lord Jesus Christ. The call of the Gospel is not to a place where everything is comfortable, everything is promised to us, and our future is absolutely laid out. But we are as Abraham, who *"went out, not knowing where he was going (Hebrews 11:8 ESV)."* We are called to risk our lives. We are staking our lives on the Word of God and the experience that God has given us in our Lord Jesus Christ.

The Bible records this willingness to risk throughout. Judges 5:18 tells us of Zebulun and Naphtali. They were a people who jeopardized their lives unto the death in defense of the land of God and the people of God. They were determined to conquer or to die; they plunged into the thickest place of the battle. They said in essence, "We're going to win, or we're going to die!"

You remember when Esther was told by her uncle Mordecai that the people of God were in danger because this wicked man Haman had passed a law that would exterminate all the Jews. He told her to go in before the king and make petition to him. Esther told him she had not been called by the king in thirty days. In those days a monarch was a man that you did not approach, even if you were married to him. To merely come into his presence without being summoned was to risk death. But Esther said, *"If I perish, I perish (Esther 4:16 NKJV)!"* She did what these others in the Bible have done. They gambled their lives.

So, the call of God is not a call to safety or to a future that is certain. It is not a call that comes with all the factors in our hands, but it is a call to risk. The Bible says of Epaphroditus, *"because for the work of Christ he came close to death, not regarding his life (Philippians 2:30 NKJV)."* This is a gambler's mentality; to put it all on one roll of the dice. God does not call us to take our finances

19

to Las Vegas and try to beat the odds. However, God does call you and I to stake our lives on the Gospel. Epaphroditus was just such a man. He staked his life for the call of the Gospel of Jesus Christ. It means a reckless courage. As a matter of fact, in the early church they had a group of people who were called The Gamblers. These were people who visited jails and desperate criminals. They ministered to those who had contagious diseases, and who were physically ill. They were disciples who went into such horrendous places to carry the Gospel, that they called them The Gamblers. They were men exactly like Paul and Barnabas, who staked their lives. At one time in Carthage, Egypt, there was a terrible plague. The officials were throwing the bodies and the carcasses of those who were dying outside the wall, and not burying them at all. Cyprian, the over-seer of the Church in Carthage, called the Christians together and rallied them to the task. The people of the church took the bodies of these diseased people and buried them. Then they began to minister to the sick and afflicted. History records that the city of Carthage was saved because Cyprian and his group of gamblers risked their lives for the cause of Jesus Christ. You see, the Gospel is a call to risk. This poem always stirs me when I read it:

> *Generations have come and gone,*
> *Drank the cup of life, then fled!*
> *Made their Eternal Record,*
> *Then joined the army of the dead!*

> *They're gone! Oh frightful words!*
> *Where, where have they quietly fled?*
> *Gone from our sight and memory,*
> *The millions of forgotten dead!*

> *Each chased his favorite phantom,*
> *In his own respective age;*
> *Or, in the light of Eternity,*
> *Carefully wrote life's sacred page.*

Time is the momentous hour,
When Eternal character is formed;
When we divest ourselves of hope,
Or, like victors, are adorned.

Ages have rolled their rusty centuries
Along through the vista of Time,
Till now has come the AWFUL HOUR,
When it's your turn to live and mine!

My Time! O dreadful thought!
My time to act! My moment to live!
Great God, in this stupendous hour,
Infinite inspiration give!

Shall I, in this fearful hour,
Break Sin's fantastic spell?
Or, with the reckless millions,
Will I BARTER Heaven for Hell?

On the volition of my will,
I can reach the Realms of Light;
Or, I can forge Infernal chains
To bind me in Eternal Night!

Author Unknown

We turn on the idiot box and get this corrupted, perverted Gospel that comes flowing through! They say things like, "If you will just receive Jesus, you are going to be a millionaire. Peace, life, and angels of God are going to constantly be your minister. You are never going to have any uncertainty, you will always know the will of God perfectly, you will never have a shortage of money, you will always have joy and blessing, and nothing will ever go wrong." These things are just not true. Living for Jesus is a call to risk. Isaiah 28:6 says that the Lord of hosts will be *"strength to those who turn back the battle at the gate* (NKJV)." The fiercest battle was always for the gates of the city. Here the prophet says that God has a special dimension of empowering for those that risk and a grace for those who will put their lives on the line. They may never go out and preach the Gospel in a foreign land or be the pastor of a church. They may not be a high profile member, but they will labor in a congregation day by day, week by week, and month by month. They will put their future on the line for the Gospel of Jesus Christ.

The Hindering Mentality

There is a play-if-safe mentality that has gripped our generation. When we play-it-safe, something happens to us on the inside that causes fear and indecision. Self-interest begins to be enthroned and our spirit becomes dominated by self-preservation.

In the business world, most of the major corporations that we know as large and successful operations have failure, after failure, after failure. They are successful not because they succeed at every task that they endeavor to do, but because they take risks. There are a multitude of corporations nobody ever heard of. They never gambled anything; they just dried up and died. In the business world, it is a game of risk. In politics we see candidates that want to play-it-safe. They campaign as if the country needs another manager instead of a leader who will declare the direction we need to go. They are afraid of saying what they truly believe and it is often difficult to know where they really stand on issues. This has come to be known as political correctness.

Our text said they *"have risked their lives for the name of our Lord Jesus Christ* (Acts 15:25 NKJV)." They stepped out into the unknown where miracles can happen. A church or an individual who always operates within the framework of the known is bound to fail. They will never see a miracle, or great blessing, or great success. They will live all of their life in mediocrity and the chances are that they will be defeated, time and time again. Beloved, to play-it-safe means that you are going to lose the very things that you are striving to hang onto. Jesus said, *"whoever desires to save his life shall lose it* (Matthew 16:25 MKJV)." God did not call us to a play-it-safe.

There are many preachers who will never preach anything controversial. They have thousands of people filling their buildings who do not know where the pastor stands on this or that. They are afraid to preach to people. They want to make sure that regardless of what people believe they can all stand together. Unfortunately, many of them will go into eternity without God because they have never heard the call to repent. The Church is not simply to be a religious gathering, we have a message. The message of Christ polarizes people and causes them to decide for it or against it. When I get through preaching I ask for a verdict. I give an altar call, an invitation to act on what has been preached. A person can accept it or reject it. There are people perhaps in every assembly who are lost and I want to give them an opportunity to be saved. You will never know the wonders of Christ until you take that step of faith. We must put the gospel out there and let people decide for it, or against it. There will be no salvation or deliverance unless we make the Gospel of Jesus Christ clear enough to make men see that they must decide for or against God. The scripture says, *"Remember Lot's wife* (Luke 17:32 KJV)." Who was Lot's wife? She was a woman that could not decide whether she wanted to go with God, or whether she wanted to live in the filth of Sodom. Sodom was familiar and represented security. The play-it-safe mentality is a hindrance.

If we are going to wait for perfect people to launch out into ministry, if we are going to wait for a perfect opportunity in a city, perfect circumstances, and until all the factors financially are in place, then we are never going to see a miracle. We are never going to see God do a work. We are called to go for broke. Our calling is to risk. The hindering mentality says to play-it-safe. The times demand it. We are living in days when inflation will eat up your savings accounts. While you are sitting there rejoicing about having a pocket full of money, it will become worthless. The times demand that you and I take action, and that we be outlandish. The times demand that we go and give our all into the work of Jesus Christ. The Devil is playing for keeps. He does not slumber or take vacations. He never misses church and if you are not in your seat, he will be there. He means business. He is playing for eternity and for eternal souls. He is going all out because he knows he has but a short time. If you have ever been in a fist fight, you know that the best way to get soundly thrashed is to keep defending yourself. Your opponent will hang one on you and he will beat you to a pulp. My daddy said, "Son don't you fight. Don't fight son, but if you have to," he said, "I want you to win. You use clubs, chains, baseball bats, or anything else. Fight as dogs and cats do: scratch, kick, and claw." Now, I always remember what my daddy told me, and when I got saved, I got a new opponent. We got a devil that means business. If you think you are just going to spar around with him a little bit I have news for you. He is loaded with brass knuckles, big rocks, and clubs. And if you are just going to kind of mess around, you may as well quit and throw in the towel, because you are whipped before you start. He knows he has but a short time and you are going to have to go for broke. This generation is going to see the coming of the Lord Jesus. If we do not avail ourselves of the opportunity, it will be lost forever.

I well remember the story of Ahithophel and Hushai. These were both counselors to King David. Ahithophel defected to Absalom, David's son. When Absalom rose up in insurrection, Hushai sided with David, but David asked him to go back and be a counselor so that he could upset the counsel of Ahithophel. While David was fleeing for his life to the Jordan River, Absalom said to Ahithophel, "What shall we do? Shall we rush after him now, or shall we wait?" Ahithophel said, "If you do not get him now while he's in disarray and upset, you will never catch him."That was good advice. However, Hushai said the opposite and convinced Absalom to wait. He lost the only opportunity available to overthrow David (2 Samuel 17:1-14).

So it is with the Church of Jesus Christ. We are living in a day when we have to go for broke. That means all or nothing. If we are just going to play it safe in the church, then we are going to lose everything that we have. I have never started to take a step of faith in church planting without having the devil and all Hell break loose. The devil says, "Go ahead man, I'm going to break you. You won't have enough money left to even pay the postage to write a letter, much less support a church." But I say, "Devil, you're a liar. God's church will survive, and God's church will reign." And every time the devil tries to bring discouragement about planting one church, I say, "Plant two! Hallelujah!!!" We live in days, when it is double or nothing, and we must do what God has called us to do.

The Overriding Confidence

We have an overriding confidence from the Word of God. As believers, one thing we know is that we cannot lose if we get in the game. Hebrews 11 should give encouragement to every one of us. In this chapter are found two groups of people. The first are those who stopped the mouths of lions, quenched the violence of fire, saw the dead raised, and who had tremendous victories. However, we also see a group of people among whom some paid with their lives, were stoned, sawn asunder, tempted, and slain with the sword. They wandered about in sheep skins being destitute, afflicted, and tormented. But, thank God, when the chapter ends both groups are in heaven. They are looking down at you and I now to see how we are going to play the game and run the race. They all won! Those who paid with their lives and those who ruled and reigned! They are all together with Him! They are sitting tonight in the great amphitheater of heaven watching us and cheering, "This is the hour, let's go! You can't lose if you just get in the game. The only ones that lose are the ones that won't play!"

A couple of our pastors and I were having lunch and we had a new convert with us. We were talking along these same lines and this new convert was listening intently because he wanted to know what preachers talk about, and what they do. We could see he was getting pretty excited. Finally, he could not stand it any longer and blurted out tremendous wisdom, "The devil may have better tricks, but we have better weapons." I said, "From the mouth of a babe comes forth the wisdom of God." He knew something that every believer should have confidence in, *"if God be for us, who can be against us* (Romans 8:31 KJV)?"

Jesus told his disciples, *"Do you not say, It is yet four months, and the harvest comes* (John 4:35 MKJV)?" He had just ministered to a little woman picked from the pits of sin. She was bruised, had been taken advantage of and used. Her life was a reproach in her city. She was divorced five times and was currently living in adultery. But Jesus touched her heart. She was moved upon by the grace of God. Such a revolution took place in her life that the whole city came out to see this man, Jesus. She was an unqualified worker. In that context, Jesus spoke these words to the disciples. He told them, *"I say to you, Lift up your eyes and look on the fields, for they are white to harvest already* (John 4:35 MKJV)." I wish we could feel what is in the heart of God for world evangelism. I wish we could feel what God feels for every little city around the world. Our hearts should not be satisfied simply to exist.

While David was in exile, one day he lifted up his voice and said, *"Oh that one would give me drink of the water of the well of Bethlehem, which is by the gate* (2 Samuel 23:15 KJV)." Three of his mighty men heard that and were so loyal to David that they risked their lives and broke through the enemy lines so they could fulfill his request. He poured it out and said, *"Be it far from me, O LORD, that I should do this: is not this the blood of the men that went in jeopardy of their lives* (2 Samuel 23:17 KJV)?" As we think of that, think of the multitudes that are without the Water of Life; multitudes who are crying out in desperation. If these men, out of loyalty to a man, would risk their lives simply to bring that water, how much more ought you and I risk who have a Savior who has given us the living water. Our Savior left heaven's glory, came down to earth, suffered, and shed blood and died. He paid the price for our sin and was buried. He rose again by the power of God. How much more ought we to take the Water of Life to those that Jesus loves and died for. I would to God that we could see that, *"if God be for us, who can be against us* (Romans 8:31 KJV)?"

Multiplication
by Wayman Mitchell

As a beginning pastor, I felt that if anybody was truly spiritual, their shoe soles had to be worn out and they should have just barely enough money to buy beans and a little hamburger to scratch by with. If you had more than that you were carnal. But God began to deal with me about some things in the Bible. I discovered that I could not defend that doctrine scripturally at all, but that God's will for me was something altogether different. As I laid hold of this and began to practice it, proclaim it, and teach it to the congregation, it has blessed me. It has blessed every church where I have been pastor.

This poverty mentality is in the thinking of a great number of Christian people. They think we are to be a little crew of moth-eaten, brow-beaten, discouraged troopers just holding out to the end. "All we can do is scratch through. Ain't nobody left, just you and me (and you're probably going down). We're just going to be martyrs for Jesus, and that's the way Christianity is meant to be." That might be your circumstance, but the Bible declares that there is another principle working, even when the situation seems bad. We need to lay hold of that and begin to believe it and practice it.

The book of Exodus tells the story of when the children of Israel were slaves in Egypt and how God began to move against Pharaoh's power to bring their deliverance. "We're going to go into the wilderness and worship God," they said to Pharaoh, but he answered, "You're not going to do any such thing. If you want to worship, worship here." They said, "No! We're going to go three days journey into the wilderness and worship." So Pharaoh said, "Okay, you can go, but you can't take any of your livestock. Leave all of it here." The people replied, "No! We're going to take all that we own. The livestock must go with us because we need them in worshiping and serving God." Pharaoh said, "Okay, you can go, but you must leave your families here." The people answered again, "No deal! We're going to go with our families and our substance." They pressed on through and would not settle for less than God wanted and the power of God broke the will of Pharaoh and they went out of Egypt (Exodus 5-12).

We are not destined in this age to just hole up somewhere and watch everything go down the tubes. I do not believe that just you and me and a little handful of three or four are going to finally make it through. I believe that we are in one of the greatest movements of the Spirit of God ever. God is gathering a people who are discovering the revelation of the scripture, and they are rising up and beginning to believe God for what their inheritance is in Christ Jesus. I believe that God would have us to know that.

When you have entered the land the LORD your God is giving you as an inheritance and have taken possession of it and settled in it, take some of the firstfruits of all that you produce from the soil of the land the LORD your God is giving you and put them in a basket. Then go to the place the LORD your God will choose as a dwelling for his Name and say to the priest in office at the time, "I declare today to the LORD your God that I have come to the land the LORD swore to our ancestors to give us." The priest shall take the basket from your hands and set it down in front of the altar of the LORD your God. Then you shall declare before the LORD your God: "My father was a wandering Aramean, and he went down into Egypt with a few people and lived there and became a great nation, powerful and numerous. But the Egyptians mistreated us and made us suffer, subjecting us to harsh labor. Then we cried out to the LORD, the God of our ancestors, and the LORD heard our voice and saw our misery, toil and oppression. So the LORD brought us out of Egypt with a mighty hand and an outstretched arm, with great terror and with signs and wonders. He brought us to this place and gave us this land, a land flowing with milk and honey; and now I bring the firstfruits of the soil that you, LORD, have given me." Place the basket before the LORD your God and bow down before him. Then you and the Levites and the foreigners residing among you shall rejoice in all the good things the LORD your God has given to you and your household. Deuteronomy 26:1-11 NIV

The Principle of Multiplication

One of the great principles of the Kingdom of God is multiplication. We can look back into the Old Testament and see a God-created humanity and a God-created world. The Lord looked upon it, blessed it and released multiplication into all that pertained to it. The Bible says, *"And God blessed them, and God said unto them, Be fruitful, and multiply, and replenish the earth, and subdue it: and have dominion over the fish of the sea, and over the fowl of the air, and over every living thing that moveth upon the earth* (Genesis 1:28 KJV)." In creation we find that God made the plants with a seed in them that they would reproduce by multiplication. God filled the oceans with fish, and in them He put the same principle of multiplication so that within themselves, they would have the capability of reproduction. In the animals we see this same principle. All of this was for the benefit of His people.

When the flood ended and Noah came out of the ark, God blessed Noah and said, *"And you be fruitful and multiply. Bring forth abundantly in the earth, and increase in it* (Genesis 9:7 KJV)." This principle of multiplication was part of the covenant God made with Noah and his descendants. This particularly concerns a man called Abraham. The Bible says, *"And he brought him outside and said, 'Look toward heaven, and number the stars, if you are able to number them.' Then he said to him, 'So shall your offspring be.' And he believed the LORD, and he counted it to him as righteousness* (Genesis 15:5-6 ESV)." When Isaac was born to Abraham, the same promise was made. God appeared to Isaac saying, "*I will multiply your offspring as the stars of heaven and will give to your offspring all these lands. And in your offspring all the nations of the earth shall be blessed* (Genesis 26:4 ESV)." To Jacob, the son of Isaac, God said, "*I will surely do you good, and make your offspring as the sand of the sea, which cannot be numbered for multitude* (Genesis 32:12 ESV)." This same promise is reiterated, coming down from creation by covenant promise through Abraham and you can follow it clear on through the lineage of David.

This is a fundamental principle of the Kingdom of God. The fruit contains the seed and God moves upon the seed in mighty blessing. The seed is called to come forth and to multiply and this is particularly expressed in God's people and the things they touch. Even in adverse conditions, this principle abides. God will make that seed grow, against all the odds. He will bless the seed and bring forth the increase by His glorious power.

We find this in the children of Israel when they were in Egypt. They went up to the land of Goshen and there they began be to be blessed of God. They were descendants of Abraham and Isaac, heirs of the promise. Jacob and his twelve sons, and their children dwelt in the land of Goshen, and as they multiplied, the Egyptians became afraid of them. They began to oppress them and lay heavy burdens upon them. They even began to take their male children and slay them (You remember the story of Moses). Yet, in spite of adverse circumstances, this principle of multiplication still operated. God says in His word that the more Egypt oppressed and afflicted them, the more Israel grew and multiplied (Exodus 1:12). Seventy souls went into Egypt and three million came out, four hundred years later.

In the Old Testament, a woman who could not have children was looked upon with reproach and believed to lack favor with God. In every case where they cried out to God asking for deliverance, God heard their prayer, healed them, and they began to bear children.

And to Abraham and to his Seed the promises were spoken. It does not say, And to seeds, as of many; but as of one, "And to your Seed," which is Christ...And if you are Christ's, then you are Abraham's seed and heirs according to the promise. Galatians 3:16 & 29 MKJV

The same powerful force that was present in the lives of Abraham's descendants and brought multiplication in the physical realm now moves through Jesus Christ to bring spiritual children. The same multiplying forces that caused Israel to be a mighty people now move in us, Abraham's spiritual heirs.

We read this prayer of confession, *"My father was a Syrian ready to perish. And he went down to Egypt, and stayed there with a few, and became there a nation, great, mighty, and many (Deuteronomy 26:5 MKJV)."* The scripture says, *"...the word of God grew and multiplied (Acts 12:24 KJV).* This multiplying principle went with them and began to work in mighty power, in a great spread of believers in Jesus Christ. The multitudes believed and the number of those who became disciples multiplied everywhere that the believers went.

The next Sabbath almost the whole city gathered to hear the word of the Lord. But when the Jews saw the crowds, they were filled with jealousy... Acts 13:44-45 ESV

And some of them believed and joined themselves to Paul and Silas, both a great multitude of the worshiping Greeks, and not a few of the chief women. Acts 17:4 MKJV

When believers will give their hearts to God through faith in Jesus Christ the multiplication principle is then released in them. Wherever they go, regardless of what nation they are in, what race, language, or financial condition, the multiplication power is released and multitudes come to the Kingdom of God. The tremendous thing is that it moves from the arithmetic to the geometric. By arithmetic, I mean one, two, three, four, and five; one gets saved and is added to the church, another and then another...thank God for the additions. One at a time is wonderful, but that will never reach the world's seven billion souls. What we need is multiplication. What we need is the promise of God that was given to Abraham that did not simply stop at physical lineage, but is applied to all who believe in God through Jesus Christ. God told Abraham to look at the skies and *"count the stars, if you are able to count them* (Genesis 15:5 MKJV)." That is the number of descendants promised; not just addition, but multiplication. Geometric means, two, four, eight, sixteen, thirty-two...before you can blink you have thousands on your hands. We have this record, *"the word of God grew and multiplied* (Acts 12:24 KJV)." Churches were established in the faith, and increased in number daily. Every day they were planting a new church.

We are satisfied if we can get a hundred people together. We say, "Glory to God, this is revival!" I am talking about something beyond our human understanding and our limited capabilities. I am talking about the miracle power of the seed. In three hundred years, this group of eleven disciples and the followers of Jesus (barely numbering 100) had so exploded in the known world that they brought the empire to its knees and Christianized the entire known world.

The Release

The scripture says these words, *"he believed the LORD* (Genesis 15:6 ESV)." Here is the key to releasing this principle. Abraham believed that God was capable, and that God would indeed perform the multiplication. Even though Abraham had no son and was one-hundred years old, he said, "God, I believe that."

33

For he who beyond hope believed on hope for him to become the father of many nations (according to that which was spoken, "So your seed shall be"). And not being weak in faith, he did not consider his own body already dead (being about a hundred years old) or the deadening of Sarah's womb. He did not stagger at the promise of God through unbelief, but was strong in faith, giving glory to God, and being fully persuaded that what God had promised, He was also able to perform. And therefore it was imputed to him for righteousness. Romans 4:18-22 MKJV

All this may sound like vague theology, so we need to bring it down to where we live. This is talking about your loved ones getting saved, people on your job, and in your neighborhood. You may say, "I don't mind believing God to save people, but you don't know my uncle, you don't know my boss, and my neighborhood is just a habitation of devils." The Bible says, *"he did not consider his own body already dead (being about a hundred years old) or the deadening of Sarah's womb* (Romans 4:19 MKJV)."

I have been the pastor of churches where if anything was going to happen, it would have to be a miracle. I looked within myself and there were no answers there. If God was going to do something, it would take something besides me. I looked at the realities and said, "God, there's no hope." The scripture says that Abraham *"beyond hope believed on hope* (Romans 4:18 MKJV)." The time of life was passed for Abraham and Sarah. This was not written for Abraham's sake at all; it was written for our benefit and instruction. Abraham, who is the father of us all, set the principle in motion. It was to him that God said, "I'm going to multiply," and it was to us, the heirs of the promise, that God said, "I'm going to multiply beyond the stars of the sky, the sand of the seashore, the dust of the earth."

If you are ever going to see this come to pass you must look to something outside yourself. You have

34

probably already discovered you do not have what it takes and even felt like throwing in the towel. Perhaps you are pioneering a church and you look out at your eight or ten saints who barely have enough faith to get out of bed on Sunday morning, and you say, "God, nothing's going to happen around here." The devil looks you in the eye and says, "That's right, nothing!" We are not talking about human ability or human principles. We are talking about God, who created seed with reproductive properties within itself. God says, "I'm going to touch that seed, and I'm going to cause it to flourish and spring up and multiply."

Abraham's Seed

You must get past the confession of failure and unbelief. All Abraham would have had to do was say, "God, I don't believe that." God would have said, "Okay, I'll find somebody else. I'll find a rock over here and raise it up." But Abraham said, "God, I believe." God said, "Abraham, you're a righteous man, and you're going to see it come to pass because of your faith."

Abraham had released into his life the multiplying principle that God began with Adam. He released it into his life and there are millions of people in the world today who are of the physical lineage of Abraham. More than that, there are multiplied millions today who are of the spiritual lineage of Abraham. Faith releases the multipliers of the Kingdom. Jesus did not say to the disciples (who were exactly like you and I), "I have chosen you and ordained you, that you should go forth and bring forth nothing but despair, hopelessness, and moth-eaten people, hiding behind the church, and holding out till the end."

You did not choose me, but I chose you and appointed you that you should go and bear fruit and that your fruit should abide, so that whatever you ask the Father in my name, he may give it to you. John 15:16 ESV

But that sown on the good ground is this: he who hears the Word and understands; who also bears fruit and produces one truly a hundredfold; and one sixty; and one thirty. Matthew 13:23 MKJV

But that sown on the good ground is this: he who hears the Word and understands; who also bears fruit and produces one truly a hundredfold; and one sixty; and one thirty. Matthew 13:23 MKJV

Jesus did not say, "Well, it isn't time yet. I don't believe anybody's ready to get saved." No, the time is now. Those people you think are not ready to get saved are ready right now. Too often we are like Abraham could have been. We look at the old shriveled up creaky body; we have a look at Sarah's womb and we say, "Nothing's going to happen around here." We say this in our own lives, we say this on our jobs, and we say this about our families. But God says that if we have faith, we can release that principle of multiplication. If you belong to Christ, you are Abraham's seed and heir according to the promise.

We read in the book of Genesis about a famine in the land (Genesis 26). Isaac, the son and heir to Abraham, was headed down to Egypt to escape the famine. As he went down, God spoke to him and said (paraphrased), "Don't go to Egypt. I didn't call you to Egypt. I called you to this land. I'm going to give you this land." Isaac said, "God, there's nothing to eat here. There's nothing growing here. I've got to go to Egypt." God said, "You stay in the land, because I have promised that I would make you fruitful and multiply you. You stay here, and I will bless you." Isaac stayed there and planted his crop in the midst of famine; while people were dying of starvation Isaac planted a crop, and it multiplied a hundred fold. God made him a wealthy man right there in the midst of famine and starvation (Genesis 26:12-14).

Adoniram Judson was a missionary in Burma who had no success in spreading the gospel. One day, after he had suffered a long series of failures, he received word from home. His supervisors timidly wrote him to ask how, under the circumstances, he viewed his prospects. His return letter said, "My prospects are as bright as the promises of God." Until that time, he had not seen one single soul brought to salvation. From that very moment on, he commenced to see thousands accept Jesus Christ throughout Burma. At the time of his death there were sixty-three churches and seven-thousand converts. His positive confession of the promises of God in the face of defeat, failure, and despair, released the explosive power of God's multiplying principle in his life, and Abraham's seed began to multiply.

We are the children of our father Abraham because we have believed in Jesus Christ. The Bible declares, *"And if you are Christ's, then you are Abraham's seed and heirs according to the promise* (Galatians 3:29 MKJV)." What if God's people rose up and began to confess that there is no impossibility with God? He can save beyond everything that we can even think of. He can multiply, because the power is not in you and I, the power is in God's seed, Jesus Christ, and Jesus Christ is capable of multiplying not only arithmetically but geometrically. This means that your family can get saved, your co-workers, and your neighbors can get saved. It means that your church, if God's people will begin to confess faith and believe God, could in six months begin to wonder, "Why on earth did we build this building so small." Do you believe that? Do you think that is just preacher's talk? I am just telling you what the Bible says. We are just toiling with ones and twos, but God has so much more.

I remember when I got out of grade school and went on to junior high, and then finally, on into high school. We graduated from the simple things like addition, into geometry (which I never did catch on to), and then to algebra which I had to take twice. I never did understand it, but just because I do not understand it does not mean it does not work. They have people that not only work geometry but trigonometry and all those things that are up to the tenth power and to the hundredth power and to the power of that power that I could not even grasp. But just because I cannot grasp it does not mean it does not work. It just simply means that in my peanut brain I am incapable of grasping it. Abraham did not have to understand it, only believe. He considered not his own body (no hope there) neither the womb of Sarah (no hope there either), but was strong in faith, giving glory to God, and confessing that which he had promised, God was also capable of performing. If God can find sons of Abraham who would begin, in the face of defeat, in the face of opposition, and in the face of failure, to quit confessing their fears and start confessing what God says, He can and will bring great multiplication.

This has practical application. I am talking about your unsaved loved ones, families, the neighbor you love, your friend on the job, or your friend that you were raised with. That person that the devil tells you will never be saved or could be saved. I want you to know God can save anyone, anywhere, and anytime. This means that when you and I begin to believe God, bind the powers of the Devil, and release the gospel's multiplying power, then families start getting healed, people start coming to Christ, souls start getting saved, lives start getting changed, and churches start getting multiplied. The Geometric principle of the Kingdom of God begins to be manifest in wonderful changed lives coming to Jesus Christ.

Hospitality
by Wayman Mitchell

There is a principle in the Bible that is one of the most powerful for reaching souls. It is a modern word that is not used very often anymore and is less seldom practiced. It is the word HOSPITALITY.

The LORD appeared to Abraham at the sacred trees of Mamre. As Abraham was sitting at the entrance of his tent during the hottest part of the day, he looked up and saw three men standing there. As soon as he saw them, he ran out to meet them. Bowing down with his face touching the ground, he said, "Sirs, please do not pass by my home without stopping; I am here to serve you. Let me bring some water for you to wash your feet; you can rest here beneath this tree. I will also bring a bit of food; it will give you strength to continue your journey. You have honored me by coming to my home, so let me serve you." They replied, "Thank you; we accept." Abraham hurried into the tent and said to Sarah, "Quick, take a sack of your best flour, and bake some bread." Then he ran to the herd and picked out a calf that was tender and fat, and gave it to a servant, who hurried to get it ready. He took some cream, some milk, and the meat, and set the food before the men. There under the tree he served them himself, and they ate. Genesis 18:1-8 GNB

The Power of Hospitality

Abraham has three strangers come by and he immediately offers to bring them food, wash their feet, and make sure they are refreshed. He tells Sarah to make some cakes for them; he goes and gets a calf and instructs servants to prepare it. This is very insightful. There is more involved than just hospitality. In this encounter God gives him insight into the future. Abraham's nephew Lot is living in Sodom and these men reveal to him that it is going to be judged. He is then given the opportunity to intercede on behalf of Lot. As you continue to read this passage, God tells of the coming Messiah, *"I will raise up for them a prophet like you from among their brothers. And I will put my words in his mouth, and he shall speak to them all that I command him. And whoever will not listen to my words that he shall speak in my name, I myself will require it of him* (Deuteronomy 18:18-19 ESV)."

Hospitality is linked to our destiny. The Old Testament emphasizes this principle. As a matter of fact I was surprised by how often this theme comes through. God gives a command that we should reach out to strangers.

And you shall rejoice in your feast, you, and your son, and your daughter, and your male slave, and your slave-girl, and the Levite, the stranger, and the fatherless, and the widow inside your gates. Deuteronomy 16:14 MKJV

At harvest time the law forbade reaping the edges of the fields. This was to be left for the poor and disadvantaged (Leviticus 23:22). This was to be a demonstration of the love of Gods people.

Do not mistreat foreigners who are living in your land. Treat them as you would an Israelite, and love them as you love yourselves. Remember that you were once foreigners in the land of Egypt. I am the LORD your God. Leviticus 19:33-34 GNB

Hospitality reveals the heart of a person. The word hospitality literally means, *"fond of guests, given to love, friendly."* The church is admonished to avail itself of the opportunity to extend hospitality.

...distributing to the needs of the saints, pursuing hospitality. Romans 12:13 MKJV

Therefore an overseer must be above reproach, the husband of one wife, sober-minded, self-controlled, respectable, hospitable, able to teach...1 Timothy 3:2 ESV

...but revealed His Word in its own times in a proclamation, with which I was entrusted by the command of God our Savior; Titus 1:3 MKJV

Show hospitality to one another without grumbling. 1 Peter 4:9 ESV

Why would people grumble about hospitality? Obviously, some people may obey God but not be very happy about it. People will complain that they serve steaks but when they are invited over only get chips and dip. It may be true, but God is emphatic that this principle be at work.

I was pastor a number of years ago in Vancouver Island, British Colombia. They had a practice there that any visitor that came to the church was approached by a member of the church and invited over for tea or some type of meal. I observed that and have imparted that into every congregation that we have ministered in. I am telling you that this will transform a church.

When my wife and I were first saved it took me about a year to lock into Christianity. I had a brother that was part of that congregation and his wife is a tremendous cook. Every Sunday she would make a roast, potatoes with gravy, and green beans with bacon grease. It is a lost art these days. I have to be honest that I went to church not so much for the Word but for the cooking after service. Eventually God worked something a little deeper than a free meal.

This principle of hospitality is powerful. It does not have to involve a full spread of food with t-bone steaks.

We are talking about the spirit of reaching out to strangers and welcoming them. There is nothing that touches people like inviting them to your house and showing them that you are really interested in them. That is what hospitality is all about.

Key Elements of Hospitality

This often does not come naturally. We live in a modern generation that is fast food, quick church, and shallow relationships. There is a church in Chandler, AZ that advertises fifteen minute services. This is the generation that does not want to take the time to do anything but selfish indulgence. The result is that many people are in isolation. They go to church but never really connect with anybody. They do nothing to reach out to others and often do not know how to make a relationship with somebody. Sometimes selfishness will dominate a person's life and they do not want to be bothered by anyone else. Sometimes a person feels inferior or insecure in presenting themselves. "*A man who isolates himself seeks his own desire; He rages against all wise judgment* (Proverbs 18:1 NKJV)." There is a spiritual, social, and relational imbalance that happens to a person who does not intentionally begin to relate to people beyond his own little circle.

The focus of hospitality is on strangers. Abraham encounters three men. He has never laid eyes on these people before but he reaches out and invites them to refresh themselves. This is the essence of hospitality. The difficulty we have today, and this is true in many churches, is that people are in what I call the purple circle. This is the in crowd, the ones that associate together. They do not intentionally convey that others are not allowed in their circle but they do not reach out and they are very partial in their relationships. People can become isolated even in a congregation and we miss the opportunity to minister to strangers and to help them feel welcome. Remember, Deuteronomy 16:14 commanded that the people of God reach out to strangers and invite them to their feasts (fellowships). Hospitality is the sincere desire to influence someone else and allow them into your life. There is a willingness to share. This is a crucial part we do not want to miss that is at the core of hospitality. It means our sustenance is shared; our time shared, home, energy, and emotions are shared.

It is intriguing how often this is at the root of events that happened in the Bible. The prophet Elijah asks the widow of Zarephath for water and a cake. Out of that willingness to minister to a stranger, God works a miracle of provision for her that keeps her through some eighteen months of famine. After a while her son falls sick and dies, but God raises him from the dead (1 Kings 17:8-24). The door is opened for a miracle of grace in the life of a woman at Shunem because of her hospitality to the prophet Elisha. She builds a room for the prophet with a bed and a candle. She constrained him to eat and stay in the room whenever he traveled in that area. The prophet inquires what he might do for her and it is revealed that she is barren. She receives a son by a miracle of God. Later that son is raised from the dead (2 Kings 4:8-37). However, there is more. She was warned by the prophet of a famine and she escaped it by going to a foreign land. Seven years pass; she returns but is now a widow and has lost her farm. Gehazi, who was the servant of Elisha, is telling the king of the miracles of God through the prophet. As he is telling the story of this woman she comes walking in to petition the king for her land. The king restores her land and the lost income from the seven years (2 Kings 8:5-6). God stores up blessing for those that are hospitable in life.

A Biblical Challenge

Hospitality is a missing ingredient for many reasons. Sometimes there is no teaching or example to follow. There perhaps is not a realization of duty of those that believe to be hospitable. Sometimes people do not appreciate the rewards that come from it. Then, of course, there is an unwillingness to be made vulnerable to people that we do not know or be inconvenienced by them. Maybe you have invited somebody over and when they left so did something valuable from your house. It happens. Any of us who have been hospitable have experienced it. Maybe somebody stained the carpet really bad or their unruly kids broke something or scratched your beautiful wood floor. I was talking to one pastor about this and he said he had a valuable china plate that had been in the family for generations. One night he had a family over and their ungoverned kids broke the plate. Those things happen.

In this story of Abraham we have a profound lesson. These strangers did not appear to be anything but weary travelers, but in actuality it was God visiting Abraham. If we fail to be hospitable we can miss God!

> *Do not neglect to show hospitality to strangers, for thereby some have entertained angels unawares. Hebrews 13:2 ESV*

According to the words of our Lord Jesus Christ this is one of the marks present in the New Testament church (John 13:35). It is interesting that the tremendous testimony of church growth in the book of Acts has in the background the spirit of hospitality.

> *And continuing with one accord in the temple, and breaking bread from house to house, they shared food with gladness and simplicity of heart, praising God and having favor with all the people. And the Lord added to the church daily those who were being saved. Acts 2:46-47 MKJV*

> *Then the King shall say to those on His right hand, Come, blessed of My Father, inherit the kingdom prepared for you from the foundation of the world. For I was hungry, and you gave me food; I was thirsty, and you gave Me drink; I was a stranger, and you took Me in; I was naked, and you clothed Me; I*

was sick, and you visited Me; I was in prison, and you came to Me. Then the righteous shall answer Him, saying, Lord, when did we see You hungry, and fed You? Or thirsty, and gave You drink? When did we see You a stranger, and took You in? Or naked, and clothed You? Or when did we see You sick, or in prison, and came to You? And the King shall answer and say to them, Truly I say to you, Inasmuch as you did it to one of the least of these My brothers, you have done it to Me. Matthew 25:34-40 MKJV

Many of the miracles in the Bible took place out of the setting of hospitality, or when a meal was being served. There is a very clear record and example in the Bible. Jesus ministered to a sinful woman in Simon the Pharisees house. This precious soul came to salvation and forgiveness of sin with hospitality as the backdrop (Luke 7:36-48). On the road to Emmaus a stranger joins with two disciples as they travel. They invited the stranger to stay with them and while they were eating Jesus reveals himself to them. Without hospitality he would have kept on going. They did not recognize him until they were eating (Luke 24:13-31). The three strangers ask Abraham after the meal, *"Where is Sarah your wife?"* Abraham and Sarah then receive the promise of a son (Genesis 18:9-10 NKJV). Out of this setting of hospitality is the atmosphere of God moving and releasing his miracle power.

One of the secrets of bringing people to a hearing of the gospel is not some fantastic speaker or personality. It happens when lonely hearts that are hungry for somebody to love them are shown hospitality. There is no greater setting than a stranger feeling accepted because he was invited for a meal. The whole world is waiting for somebody to show them some interest. People do not come to church generally because they are just dying to hear somebody preach. They come because they are lonely, feel disenfranchised, and have a genuine need. It is the spirit of reaching out and touching strangers that moves the human heart with the gospel.

Impartation
by Greg Mitchell

On May 8th, 1936, a horse jockey named Ralph Neves was riding in the third race of the day at Bay Meadows Racecourse near San Francisco, California. At stake were five-hundred dollars cash and a gold watch that Bing Crosby had promised to personally present to the meet's winner.

Nineteen-year-old Neves (a.k.a. "the Portuguese Pepperpot") was riding Fannikins, and the two were in fifth place as he headed into the first turn behind a wall of four horses. As the horses in front of him pounded around the corner, the outside horse stumbled and fell against the horse beside it, causing a domino effect which brought all four of the leading horses down. Fannikins tripped when she tried to stop abruptly, which dumped Neves onto the track just before her crushing weight landed on top of him.

Track physicians rushed to Neves' unmoving body, and loaded him into a pickup truck to shuttle him to the track's first aid room. There, he was examined by a doctor, and pronounced dead. The track's stunned spectators observed a moment of silence when the race announcer shared the solemn news with the crowd. But they had not seen the last of Ralph Neves.

By the time Neves' friend Dr. Horace Stevens arrived at the track hospital, the jockey's bloodied body was laid out on a slab with his toe tagged for the morgue. In a desperate, long-shot attempt to revive his friend, Dr. Stevens administered a shot of adrenaline directly into Neves' heart. For several minutes it appeared to have no effect, and the discouraged Dr. Stevens left the hospital.

Sometime in the next twenty minutes, Neves sat up and walked out of the first aid room. He headed across the grandstand towards the jockeys' room, wearing nothing but his pants and one boot. When the crowd realized that the shirtless, bloodied, toe-tagged man who was staggering across the grandstand area was the jockey who had been declared dead about a half hour earlier, the crowd and the race officials rushed towards Neves. Shock turned to celebration.

Upon arriving at the jockeys' room, where his colleagues were conducting a collection for his widow, Ralph Neves demanded to be allowed to ride the rest of his races. The astonished stewards refused to let him return to riding until he spent a night in the hospital under observation. In the morning, he left the hospital through the window in his room, dressed in a hospital gown, and took a cab back to the racetrack.

He resumed his racing to finish out the last day of the meet, and though he didn't win any of his races, he did rack up enough second place finishes to capture the title and the watch. The headline on the story in the San Francisco Chronicle read: "Ralph Neves – Died but Lives, to Ride and Win." Neves went on to ride for twenty-eight more years after being declared dead in 1936.

His friend put something in Ralph Neves that caused him to live – and helped determine his future. That is a picture of what the Bible calls impartation. We have the power to receive from a man of God something that will bring life to us as disciples, and we have the power to put things in other people, as pastors, parents, and teachers.

First, I thank my God through Jesus Christ for you all, that your faith is spoken of throughout the whole world. For God is my witness, whom I serve with my spirit in the gospel of His Son, that without ceasing I make mention of you always in my prayers, making request if, by some means, now at last I may find a way in the will of God to come to you. For I long to see you, that I may impart to you some spiritual gift, so that you may be established-- that is, that I may be encouraged together with you by the mutual faith both of you and me. Romans 1:8-12 NKJV

The Truth of Transference

The Bible declares that we are spiritual creatures. There is a part of us that is supernatural called our spirit. Every person has a spirit about them. This means that when you make choices and take actions repeatedly it will become the prominent spiritual characteristic of your life. This is true for bad or good. People who are perverted and have an unclean spirit are that way because they have repeatedly given themselves to immoral behavior. You have heard somebody referred to as having a kind or gentle spirit describing the nature or demeanor of that individual.

Paul writes to the church at Rome, *"For I long to see you, that I may impart to you some spiritual gift to strengthen you* (Romans 1:11 ESV)." This scripture is talking about the good sense of impartation. There is a motivating passion, a power, and an outlook that can be put into other people. This is a powerful truth called transference of spirit. That means that what is in one person can be transferred to another person or persons. Paul wants to impart something. Impart means to give over or to share. Paul is confident that what he has inside him he can put in them.

Moses had supernatural leadership ability and God took that and imparted it to the seventy elders so they too could fulfill a leadership role (Numbers 11:25). Elisha told Elijah he wanted a double portion of his spirit (2 Kings 2:9). He was not looking for some tips or techniques about how to be a man of God. He recognized that there was something supernatural in the life of Elijah and he wanted that to be a part of his life. After Elijah departed in a whirlwind, the spirit of Elijah rested on Elisha (2 Kings 2:15).

So think about this; a spirit can be transferred or imparted. This is a powerful dimension for good. What does this mean?

Impartation involves a supernatural equipping: This brings an enablement for the circumstances of life. Paul said he wanted to impart a spiritual gift to strengthen the believers in Rome (Romans 1:11). The church in Rome was being persecuted, hounded, and killed for being believers. Paul says I can impart something that will enable you to stand.

The book *In Harm's Way*, by Doug Stanton recounts the sinking of the USS Indianapolis in the closing days of WWII. Nine-hundred-twenty-five men from the ship survived the initial sinking in shark infested waters and they clung onto bits and pieces of the ship and rafts. For four days they endured no food or water, exposure to sun, the affect of salt water on their skin, and the screams from fellow soldiers who were being eaten by sharks. One survivor described the despair that set in and how many began to give up, let go of the rafts, and drift away to drown or be eaten. He was watching one young man who was probably seventeen or eighteen and he could tell he was about to give up. Sure enough, he let go and began to drift when all of a sudden this boys says, "No! My dad says you never give up!" So he swam back and grabbed on to the raft again and it was only a few hours later that they were all rescued. Little did that father know when he was teaching his son to never give up that those words he put in him were literally going to save his life. This is the equipping of impartation.

Impartation brings motivation or passion: The two disciples on the road to Emmaus said, "*Did not our hearts burn within us while he talked to us on the road, while he opened to us the Scriptures* (Luke 24:32 ESV)?" What they are describing here is not head knowledge but something that was happening on the inside that transformed them. They were discouraged but are now seeing things from a different perspective and are therefore acting accordingly. Why? Revival is a spirit, a passion, a contagion that is caught through a man of God when he is on fire. It is more than information they are learning, it is a spirit; it is passed on from heart to heart.

Impartation brings a proper outlook or viewpoint when you are faced with obstacles and difficulties. Elijah told Elisha he could have the double portion if he stuck with him. But when Elijah was taken up and Elisha is ready to begin his ministry, he is on the wrong side of the Jordon River without a boat. Rather than crawl into a fetal position looking at his problems and caving into pressure, he rolled up the mantle and said, *"Where is the Lord, the God of Elijah* (2 Kings 2:15)?" He struck the water and the water parted. Where did he get that? He got that from Elijah, his pastor, who was not a whiner that always complained about how hard it was.

Tom Payne tells the story of early in his ministry in Las Vegas when there was a terrible rain storm and his building was flooded. It was a Wednesday afternoon and there was no way the building could be cleaned up on time for service. One of the other fellowship pastors in the area told him to cancel service and bring the people over to his church. But Tom said, "No, this flood is an assault from hell. We have to do something to the Devil just out of principle." So he called the men of his church to spread the word that they were going to show a movie in an apartment complex. They made some cheesy fliers and knocked on doors to invite the neighbors. The church was only running twenty people at the time, but that night they had sixty visitors and eleven souls saved. Tom has a way of looking at problems that he got from his pastor. That is what happens in impartation.

This is the critical factor in discipleship. This is why Jesus did not give his disciples an instruction manual to learn from, but rather said, *"Follow me* (Matthew 9:9 KJV)." There must be more than a transfer of information. Truth is more caught than taught. Disciples take on the spirit of their pastor. That is the potential of discipleship.

How Impartation Comes

Impartation is automatic; it happens whether you want it to or not. Every pastor has people in his church that frustrate him. A common statement you hear, "I can't get these people to pray, or give," or whatever. Regardless of how good your church is you will always have some people that will not get with the program. The problem is when a pastor says, "My *whole* church won't pray, or give." The pastor might come to the conclusion that these are just bad people. He can be in a big city and five blocks away his fellow pastor has good people, but somehow he got the bad ones. His fellow pastor has good disciples who are on fire for God, but his disciples are all duds. In some cases we have had pastors who want to leave their post and move to where there are good people, only to find that people are the same everywhere. The truth is that we minister what we <u>are</u>! Our congregations will reflect who we are and not who we pretend to be or who we say we are in sermons.

> *So affectionately longing for you, we were willing to have imparted to you, not only the gospel of God, but also our own souls... 1 Thessolonians 2:8 MKJV*

This is what happens in true Holy Ghost ministry. Something comes across of our own soul. We have to be honest, the reason why sometimes there is something missing in those following is because it is missing in us as leaders. Years ago, I remember Pastor Mitchell getting a phone call and I was in the room hearing his side of the conversation. A pastor on the other end was complaining that he could not get his people to give. Pastor asked all the standard questions, "Are you taking offerings? Are you preaching on money? Are you challenging the people to give?" So finally he asked the question, "Are you tithing?" There was silence! The <u>pastor</u> was not tithing! Nobody knew this man was not tithing. The congregation did not know it, but every time he talked about tithing they were not hearing or receiving what he had to say. Regardless of what he said, his true person was being imparted. Impartation happens whether you want it to or not.

Impartation comes through example. Truth must be made flesh; it has to be seen. God is truth but came to earth in the flesh so we could have an example to model ourselves after. Paul said to the church at Corinth, *"Imitate me, just as I imitate Christ* (1 Corinthians 11:1 NKJV)."

...not domineering over those in your charge, but being examples to the flock. 1 Peter 5:3 ESV

The word Peter uses for *example* is a picture of molding metal. When you pour in the metal it takes the shape of the dye and then hardens. The people you minister to will take your shape and become like you spiritually. That means we will never get people to rise above our own example. It is possible that our actions negate our words. We can show people that what we say is not to be taken seriously because of how we live. Charles Spurgeon said, "A man's life is always more forcible than his speech. When men take stock of him they reckon his deeds as dollars and his words as pennies. If his life and doctrine disagree, the mass of onlookers accept his practice and reject his preaching."

Many years ago my wife and I were visiting a congregation. My wife went back to see a friend in the nursery and she overheard a lady ask another what the pastor had preached about. The response was, "Oh, it was a good sermon, but what a pity he doesn't do any of it." The words were right, true, and from the Bible, but he did not live it so it made no impact because the people saw a contradiction. Someone said, "Advice can be confusing, but an example is clear."

Impartation comes by deliberate deposit. *And the things that thou hast heard of me among many witnesses, the same commit thou to faithful men, who shall be able to teach others also* (2 Timothy 2:2 (KJV). The word *commit* means to make a deposit; not just anything, but the same things you heard from me.

This was Jesus' method with his disciples. He taught them about true leadership, about priorities in ministry, how to deal with failure, success, and rejection, and how to use money. He taught them these lessons because he was equipping them with what they needed for the future.

...for I did not shrink from declaring to you the whole counsel of God. Acts 20:27 ESV

This is what making disciples is all about. I am constantly asking myself, "What do these men need right now? What mistakes have I made that I can help them to avoid? What do I wish I knew when I went into the ministry that I can deposit in them? What kinds of things hurt men in the ministry or help them?" I am making a deliberate deposit much like parenting. Parenting is more than wiping noses and getting them to school on time. A good parent is making an impartation in their child, equipping them for life, and teaching them a proper viewpoint in order for them to be successful.

The Choices In Impartation
There is the personal responsibility of the imparter. If you are the one doing the imparting it is your responsibility to insure that the example you are setting is worth following. You have to understand how powerful this principle is and take it seriously. Each of us has that responsibility to our children and to our spouses. Some men get bad reactions from their wives when they announce some adventure they want to take for God. Why? She does not leap with joy because she has seen the man's example and it has not exactly inspired faith.

In 2008, off the coast of Singapore, a newly trained scuba diver who was on his first dive died in a freak accident. His body was found floating in the sea with his tank still strapped to his body. The tank was found to have traces of carbon monoxide and hydrogen sulfide. This man, Mr. Sue, took his tank from the instructor in good faith and yet he was sucking in something that was killing him.

This is a responsibility we have as disciple makers. Jesus sent out his disciples and instructed them not to take a money bag, two coats, and the like (Mathew 10:9-10). Have you ever wondered what that was about? The Message translation puts it this way, "You don't need a lot of equipment. You are the equipment." I have heard men say over the years, "Man, I could have revival if they sent me out with a better sound system." The most powerful piece of equipment you possess is you! If you have got it on the inside it does not matter about the PA!

Keep a close watch on yourself and on the teaching. Persist in this, for by so doing you will save both yourself and your hearers. 1 Timothy 4:16 ESV

The person being imparted to also has a responsibility. Some will use this truth of impartation as an excuse for their lack. I wish every pastor was stellar and righteous, but they are not. So what do you do if that is your situation? I had a pastor for a couple of years who didn't really pray, read his Bible, or preach new sermons (he preached mostly borrowed sermons), and spent a lot of time watching movies. Should I then make excuse and blame him for any of my faults? That is not going to wash with God. Through that example I learned what not to be!

Everybody needs to learn the skills of accepting and rejecting. You accept what is good and reject what is bad. You chew on the meat and spit out the bones. Do not spend your years blaming the way you were raised. You have the ability and the responsibility to make wise choices. No one can do that for you.

On the other hand, don't be gullible. Check out everything, and keep only what's good. Throw out anything tainted with evil. 1 Thessalonians 5:21-22 MSG

We must lay hold of a good impartation. Not everyone who sits under righteous ministry catches the spirit. The disciple has a choice. Elijah said, "What do you want?" This is a blank check. Elisha could have asked for money, fame, or power. However, Elisha said, *"Please let a double portion of your spirit be upon me* (2 Kings 2:9 NKJV)." Elijah then proceeded to test him to see if he would be diverted. Life will have tests. Elisha received something the sons of the prophets did not. They had the necessary information in their heads, but Elisha got the spirit. He had heart and passion. There are men in every church who know lots of stuff but they do not catch the fire. They never get it because there is nothing in them that says, "God that is what I want." We are responsible to:

Ask God for it. (Mathew 7:7-8)

Ask questions. It is amazing that disciples will be around men who have tremendous experience and yet not ask questions. They crack jokes, talk politics and sports, and yet they do not take advantage of the opportunity. You can't think of questions at the time? Write down your questions for when you have the opportunity. I tell people they will never bother me by asking a question because discipleship is my priority.

Think. Why do we do it like that? Many never wonder or think things through until some religious nut challenges them and then they conform because of lack of conviction and principle.

Seek to reproduce it. Are you reproducing the spirit of your pastor, the spirit of our fellowship?

Let me leave you with some encouragement. For some people, the truth of impartation leaves them feeling doomed. Some, because they feel they missed out by not sitting under this or that pastor's ministry. **God can give you something worth imparting.** It's available!

> *Cry out for wisdom, and beg for understanding. Search for it like silver, and hunt for it like hidden treasure. Then you will understand respect for the Lord, and you will find that you know God. Proverbs 2:3-5 NCV*

Some feel doomed because they have made terrible mistakes and have set a bad example for their wife, children and disciples. **God can restore something worth imparting.** He can restore what has been lost. If the fire and a passion to do the will of God has dimmed; if you have drifted and allowed other things to take priority in front of God; if you can recognize that then there is hope. God is not waiting to squash you and throw you into hell. Instead he can stir that to life again.

For this reason I remind you to fan into flame the gift of God, which is in you through the laying on of my hands. 2 Timothy 1:6 ESV

You can get it back again. You can cry out to the God who put the fire there in the first place. The Bible says, "*A bruised reed he will not break, and a smoking flax he will not quench* (Matthew 12:20 NKJV)." God sees the fire that is barely flickering and He can blow on the embers and bring it to life in you again.

Largeness of Heart
by Wayman Mitchell

I was in Tucson for a crusade on the rodeo grounds and there were a couple of teams of newspaper cameramen. I never get too excited about being in the paper because you never know what kind of spin they will put on what is taking place. Several people were healed and I told the cameramen to make sure they get pictures; but of course they put pictures of people who did not get healed. The article was not too bad, but the bottom line conclusion of these reporters was that we were just reaching a bunch of Mexicans.

My wife and I were the pastors of a church in Eugene, OR years back and our church was just below a very upscale part of the city where some wealthy people lived. A visitor from this area came to one of our events and she was overheard to say, "There is just a bunch of poor people in here."

Many people when they come into our churches are looking for some spiritual body building material. Spiritually speaking, all they see is a bunch of scrawny legged Christian folks with a caved in chest who are in the process of being made disciples. They are not very impressed. But the issue is not what we are but what we can become. Regardless of what race you are, social status, or who you are today, the final verdict is not here and now but what we can become in the future.

And coming into the parts of Caesarea Philippi, Jesus asked His disciples, saying, Who do men say Me to be, the Son of Man? And they said, Some say, John the Baptist; some, Elijah; and others, Jeremiah, or one of the prophets. He said to them, But who do you say I am? And Simon Peter answered and said, You are the Christ, the Son of the living God. Jesus answered and said to him, You are blessed, Simon, son of Jonah, for flesh and blood did not reveal it to you, but

*My Father in Heaven. And I also say to you that you
are Peter, and on this rock I will build My church,
and the gates of hell shall not prevail against it.
Matthew 16:13-18 MKJV*

These verses give us tremendous insight. Jesus said,
"you are Peter (Greek word Petros = a little stone) *and on
this rock* (Greek word Petra = massive rock) *I will build my
church."* He was not speaking what Peter was, but what
Peter was going to become. We all know that Peter failed
miserably in the denial of the Lord Jesus Christ on the
night of the crucifixion. So Jesus was speaking of what
Peter would become after the failure and restoration. This
is the message of the gospel; what we can become in God.

The key to releasing God's potential is in this text.
The key is largeness of heart in disciple makers. A
synonym we could use is *magnanimity.*

The Call to Largeness of Heart (Magnanimity)
This does not come naturally. The reason is because
we are fallen humanity. You know the story in the
garden, Adam and Eve disobeyed God and self-interest
is the curse of that decision. The devil told them that if
they would partake of the fruit they were going to
become gods. Something happened in that decision and
self-idolatry replaced God in their hearts. This has
tainted all of us with what could be called small
mindedness. That means that we never see beyond our
own self-interest naturally. It has been said that you can
tell the character of a man by how he treats those who
can do nothing to him or for him. The call is to largeness
of heart and this is rooted in compassion.

*Christ himself carried our sins in his body to the
cross, so that we might die to sin and live for
righteousness. It is by his wounds that you have been
healed. 1 Peter 2:24 GNB*

Definition of largeness of heart: Large minded, large hearted, generous disposition, noble, liberal, and a synonym is a great soul or a heart large enough not to hold grudges. Largeness of heart is the ability to have grace when another person is made vulnerable. It was Spurgeon who often said, "Every man ought to cultivate a blind eye and a blind ear." In part, it is the ability to pass over a matter. Largeness of heart is the key to making disciples.

> Don't pay attention to everything people say---you may hear your servant insulting you, and you know yourself that you have insulted other people many times. *Ecclesiastes 7:21-22 GNB*

Small mindedness is the opposite: lacking tolerance, lacking breadth of vision; it produces a man that is partial and that is judgmental, narrow minded and cannot pass over a matter. Some leaders and pastors feel like they can say anything about anyone because they are in a position of authority. But if the little guy says anything of criticism about them, then they are labeled a rebel and a gossip. Isn't that an interesting facet of human personality? It is small mindedness. They cannot see beyond what a person is at the moment. If they are offended, something is said about them, if they are criticized, or if somebody does not dance their tune, then they cannot over look that. If they find a flaw in somebody else, then they must deal with that immediately; they must call that out and deal with that person. They cannot see beyond it to what a person can become.

> When the servant of the man of God rose early in the morning and went out, behold, an army with horses and chariots was all around the city. And the servant said, "Alas, my master! What shall we do?" He said, "Do not be afraid, for those who are with us are more than those who are with them." Then Elisha prayed

60

and said, "O LORD, please open his eyes that he may see." So the LORD opened the eyes of the young man, and he saw, and behold, the mountain was full of horses and chariots of fire all around Elisha. And when the Syrians came down against him, Elisha prayed to the LORD and said, "Please strike this people with blindness." So he struck them with blindness in accordance with the prayer of Elisha. And Elisha said to them, "This is not the way, and this is not the city. Follow me, and I will bring you to the man whom you seek." And he led them to Samaria. As soon as they entered Samaria, Elisha said, "O LORD, open the eyes of these men, that they may see." So the LORD opened their eyes and they saw, and behold, they were in the midst of Samaria. As soon as the king of Israel saw them, he said to Elisha, "My father, shall I strike them down? Shall I strike them down?" He answered, "You shall not strike them down. Would you strike down those whom you have taken captive with your sword and with your bow? Set bread and water before them, that they may eat and drink and go to their master." So he prepared for them a great feast, and when they had eaten and drunk, he sent them away, and they went to their master. And the Syrians did not come again on raids into the land of Israel. 2 Kings 6:15-23 ESV

Here in this text we see an army of men who have come down to kill Elisha. That army was not there just to do practice maneuvers. Somebody fingered Elisha as the man who every time the Syrians made a battle plan he would tell the king in Samaria exactly what was going to happen (2 Kings 6:11-12). Elisha leads them right into the city of Samaria and delivers them to the king. And the Bible says these tremendous words about the reaction of Elisha, *"You shall not strike them down* (2 Kings 6:22 ESV)." What a tremendous expression of grace.

Paul writes to the church at Corinth and rebukes smallness of heart.

O Corinthians, our mouth is opened to you, our heart has been enlarged. You are not restrained in us, but you are restrained in your own affections. But for the same reward, (I speak as to children), you also be enlarged. 2 Corinthians 6:11-13 MKJV

Paul says they are narrow minded, small hearted...he tells them, *"we have been large toward you but you have been narrow towards us."* He instructs us...

Let each of you look not only to his own interests, but also to the interests of others... For they all seek their own interests, not those of Jesus Christ. Philippians 2:4 &21 ESV

One day Ham goes looking for his father; Noah is drunker than a skunk and he is crashed out in his tent naked. Ham finds him, but rather than feel compassion and mercy for his father he mocks him for his failure. He does not cover him with a blanket and keep his mouth shut, but goes and tells his brothers about what he saw (Genesis 9:21-23). Have you ever noticed how cruel children can be? Some poor child has to wear glasses when he is seven years old and immediately he is called four eyes and other names. Any flaw or injury is not viewed with compassion but made the butt of their jokes and criticism. That is children; when we come to adulthood it is far more serious when you and I cannot pass over a matter. Ham was cursed for his actions (Genesis 9:24-25). Elisha passed over a matter and he exemplified the living God in grace. If you want to make disciples you are going to have to understand what largeness of heart is...the ability to see past shortcomings to what people can become.

The Crucial Issue

Small minded men cannot see beyond themselves. They cannot see beyond the present state of people's circumstances because they are more concerned with their own ego. If they are challenged by anybody in their church or if somebody they have assigned a task fails or does not perform up to expectation, then that is a direct assault to their ego. All they can see is people's shortcomings and mistakes. The small hearted will take advantage of somebody else's vulnerabilities to promote themselves. A small minded person cannot handle any dissent.

The disciples see somebody that is casting out demons in the name of Jesus and they are not a part of their little group. They go to Jesus and ask if they should call down fire on them like Elijah did the false prophets (Luke 9:54)...full of love. The small minded person sees a position they may have as an opportunity for self-exaltation. They are continually protecting their image and defending their position.

Every event of life is an intersection. How we handle that event determines how the future plays out. And so we have a revelation: future impact is made by our choices and attitude. Elisha would not kill the Syrian army and that decision affected the future because, "*the Syrians did not come again on raids into the land of Israel* (2 Kings 6:23 ESV)." Think about that. They changed the course of a nation by the decision that they made. The issue is largeness of heart. Men who do not have a large heart cannot make disciples. The reason is that they have no vision for the future; they are always dealing in the present. They cannot pass over a matter. The slightest infraction, deviation, flaw, or idiosyncrasy they have to make into a major issue. What is important to them is their ego. This has a negative impact on the person they are trying to disciple. The future of that person, what they can become, is not considered. This nullifies the discipleship process.

And I will very gladly spend and be spent for your souls, even if loving you more and more, I am loved the less. 2 Corinthians 12:15 MKJV

Paul was a great disciple maker because he had vision for seeing Christ formed in people. Embryo disciples are absent of elements that qualify them for ministry. Many people do not understand that. They are always looking for the perfect disciple. That is why they never make any disciples and they never plant any churches. They cannot find any perfect people to plant. The issue is they do not have a large enough heart to see what people can become. When Jesus told Peter these words he already knew that Peter was headed for a failure. Yet he tells him he is going to be a strong rock one day. This is what you are going to become. He was not saying what Peter was now, but what he was going to be. Largeness of heart allows us to see beyond the present short comings in a person to what a man can become. The reason many cannot make disciples is because they cannot pass over a matter. They have no largeness of heart. They do not understand that the future is the issue not the present.

We see many examples in scripture:

And every man in distress, and every man who had a creditor, and every man bitter of soul, gathered themselves to him. And he became commander over them. And about four hundred men were with him. 1 Samuel 22:2 MKJV

David was a fugitive on the run from Saul. Many men came and joined with him. They were men who had grievances, baggage, and were a mess. Out of these four-hundred men came the thirty-seven mighty men who did such great exploits in Israel (2 Samuel 23:8-39). They started out as a bunch of rejects, but David saw past that and accepted them and became their captain.

Then the people said to Samuel, "Who is it that said, 'Shall Saul reign over us?' Bring the men, that we may put them to death." But Saul said, "Not a man shall be put to death this day, for today the LORD has worked salvation in Israel." 1 Samuel 11:12-13 ESV

And David came to the two hundred who were too exhausted to follow David, whom they had made also to stay at the brook Besor. And they went out to meet David, and to meet the people with him. And David came up to the people, and greeted them. And every evil and worthless man of the men who went with David answered and said, Because they did not go with us, we will not give them from a thing the spoil that we have seized, except to every man his wife and his sons. Let them take them, and go. And David said, My brothers, you shall not do so with that which Jehovah has given us. For He has protected us, and has delivered into our hand the company that came against us. For who will listen to you in this matter? But as his part is that goes down to the battle, so shall be his part that stays by the stuff. They shall divide alike. 1 Samuel 30:21-24 MKJV

The Lord...is longsuffering toward us, not willing that any should perish but that all should come to repentance. 2 Peter 3:9 NKJV

It is in his nature to deal with souls. In making disciples we must have a continued involvement in lives looking toward their future. Too often we put God out of the equation. In our wisdom and genius we think we can rightly discern people's hearts and situations that arise. We run our churches like a business and make personnel decisions based on talent and ability. We forget that God is involved and that he cares about people. We need to give God time to work in any circumstance or affair.

I gave her time to repent... Revelation 2:21 ESV

The Key to Largeness of Heart

How you view people is the key. We have the classic story in the Old Testament of Rehoboam. He becomes king after his father Solomon. The people came to him and requested a lighter burden. Rehoboam tells them to return after a few days for an answer. Meanwhile, he consults with the elders who advised his father and they told him he should listen and speak kindly to them. If he did this they would serve him gladly forever (1 Kings 12:1-7). But Rehoboam had a small heart. He was like a pastor appointed to a church that he did not labor for but views himself as the head dude. He did not win those people; he did not bring them into the church, but now he is the man put in charge and so he is going to throw his weight around a little bit. Rehoboam wants a second opinion so he talks with the young men he grew up with.

And the young men who had grown up with him said to him, "Thus shall you speak to this people who said to you, 'Your father made our yoke heavy, but you lighten it for us,' thus shall you say to them, 'My little finger is thicker than my father's thighs. And now, whereas my father laid on you a heavy yoke, I will add to your yoke. My father disciplined you with whips, but I will discipline you with scorpions.'" 1 Kings 12:10-11 ESV

He did not listen to the heart of the people. He was pushing his own agenda and he made a fatal mistake that cost him his ministry and his kingdom (1 Kings 12:19-20). People are very valuable to God. We had a pastor who was just starting out and he had some folks that had joined with him. While they were laboring to get the building ready this pastor goes on holiday. It's like he said to them, "Hey you slobs get that building ready, I'm going on vacation." That is how you lose a ministry.

These people work full time jobs and are volunteering their time to help the church. Do you know what a volunteer is? It means they do not have to come to church; they do not have to go to your church. Some view people like merchandise to be bartered for ego gratification.

If you are a leader, God has appointed and assigned you to help people become what he wants them to be. There are no perfect people that are going to come into your church. If they come in and they look really good they will usually cause you a world of trouble. Make your own converts. Give me a drug addict or a prostitute; somebody out of the gutter of life and let the Word of God shape them and mold them.

The key to largeness of heart is a focus on serving others. Elisha served these men and put meat and drinks before them. He had them surrounded in the middle of Samaria. They were totally vulnerable and he would have been fully justified to give the order to kill them. They were dead men. These people have come to assassinate him but rather than retaliate he puts the steaks on and breaks out with the frijoles and tortillas. After the buffet he tells them they are free and sends them back home. This was a God given dimension. Largeness of heart does not come automatically nor does it come easily. In the fall of man self was enthroned. We need something beyond ourselves if we are going to have largeness of heart.

And give to Your servant an understanding heart, to judge Your people, to discern between good and bad. For who is able to judge this, Your great people? 1 Kings 3:9 MKJV

We have in these verses significant imagery. Solomon did not possess this naturally but prayed for a genuine concern and heart for God's people. He is asking that his heart be stretched. In sports they have discovered that when a muscle is stretched it can function to its full potential and capacity. This is painful and time consuming. As you watch athletes that are preparing to compete they go through the exercises of stretching. They are doing that so they can reach their full potential. It takes time, it is painful, but it is essential. Especially as they get older. I go to prayer every morning and I kneel or sit on platform while I'm praying. There was a day when the minute I was through I could spring up and go. I notice I'm moving a little slower these days. Those muscles as you get older are not as elastic as they were when you were young. This is true also in the spiritual realm. The older you get the less apt you are to have a stretched heart to be able to deal with people. You become narrow minded. This is a tremendous danger for older pastors…people become dispensable. We need God to help us.

> *And God gave Solomon exceeding great wisdom and understanding, and largeness of heart, even as the sand that is on the seashore. 1 Kings 4:29 MKJV*

> *Then thou shalt see, and flow together, and thine heart shall fear, and be enlarged… Isaiah 60:5 KJV*

Largeness of heart is linked to your attitude toward people and how you treat them. Your treatment of people releases God's potential to move through you and touch lives. Peter failed miserably in denying the Lord three times. He now sees himself as vulnerable. He had been so confident in himself, but now his heart was ready to be enlarged. Jesus finds the disciples fishing and he tells Peter three times, *"feed my sheep* (John 21:15-17)." From a failing disciple, a flawed human being like you and I, there comes a man that impacted three-thousand souls in one sermon (Acts 2:41). Something happened to Peter; a supernatural dimension beyond mechanics has transformed his heart. Out of the failure he now has an understanding of God's interest in people. There is now a largeness of heart that has enabled Peter to reach the souls of men.

Abraham Lincoln's secretary of war was Edwin Stanton. He ridiculed Lincoln, insulted him and was a constant critic. He called him an idiot and the original gorilla. Someone came one day and told Mr. Lincoln that Stanton had called him a fool for an order he had issued concerning troop movement. "If Stanton said I was a d--d fool, then I must be one, for he is nearly always right, and generally says what he means. I will step over and see him." Lincoln refused to rise because he had a large heart. Mr. Stanton became one of Lincoln's greatest allies. At Lincoln's funeral he gave a eulogy and said, "There lies one of the greatest men who ever lived."

You want a big church. You want to preach and have people respond. You want to make an impact. Largeness of heart is a must.

Isolation
by Wayman Mitchell

Whoever isolates himself seeks his own desire; he breaks out against all sound judgment. A fool takes no pleasure in understanding, but only in expressing his opinion. Proverbs 18:1-2 ESV

In the book *Sane in Damascus* by Amnon Sharon, the author talks about being a tank commander in the Yom Kippur war and being taken prisoner by the Syrians. He spent much of his imprisonment in solitary confinement, being tortured multiple times every day and he writes the book to document the various facets that he went through.

There are people who are in a self-imposed solitary confinement because of their personality. Because of the way they process life and view the world they torture themselves in their own mind and live a life of isolation. In the book *Deep Church* by Jim Belcher, he contrasts the traditional churches that are very large and have little personal relationships with what he calls the emerging church, which is generally a small group that is more intimate and allows for dialogue. He states that people are being drawn to these groups because they want something more personal rather than the isolation they feel in the larger, more formal church setting.

There is quite a trend today towards individualism. The rugged individual is spot-lighted and personal goals, desires, and pursuits are encouraged. Of course, this has its place, but there is tremendous focus on individuals who have some kind of talent or outstanding ability. Books, movies, and the sports world all highlight the hero who saves the day by their talent. I read somewhere, "The best description of humanity today is a man sitting watching T.V." People are disconnected from reality and absorbed in their own world. We could add to that the internet. The only relationship many people have is with the computer, communicating with people they have never met and are more than likely lying about who they are anyway. God did not create us for a life without relationships. You must understand that or you will miss the entire point of what God has intended for you. He designed you and me as social creatures with the ability to communicate for a reason.

Father of the fatherless and protector of widows is God in his holy habitation. God settles the solitary in a home... Psalms 68:5-6 ESV

God created the church to be a community. However, life tends to isolate us and derail us from God's original purpose. The Hebrew word for isolation is actually talking about someone who either is divisive or reclusive. Many times families impute this to their children because of prejudice. I was raised in Prescott, Arizona, which is a little red-neck city. But, we were raised with Hispanics and just took for granted there are other kinds of people in the world. I remember many years ago in the military, I was stationed in Illinois. There were some folks from the south and they considered everyone from above the Mason-Dixon Yankees. I had never experienced such prejudice in my life. They were still fighting the Civil War. We were in chow line one time and a great big guy from Kentucky went down to the front of the line and grabbed a black soldier and threw him out of the line and told him to get back where he belonged. He was trained that way because of how he was raised. People are divided and isolated because of preconceived ideas about others.

Many times in life there are events that cause an individual to begin isolating themselves. Tragedy, for example, often produces isolation. It could be the loss of a loved one, a failure of a marriage, or a betrayal in a relationship. Perhaps a disappointment in life, in the church, or in a ministry of a church, can cause somebody to become disillusioned. Sickness and disease sometimes leads to self-pity which often accompanies isolation. In order to affectively process life we must stay connected with people. However, many tend to become withdrawn.

When a person is isolated their judgment becomes skewed. Our text in Proverbs says, "*...he breaks out against all sound judgment.*" There is an unhealthy mental process that begins to take place; an imbalance in emotion and perspective. People who are isolated become introspective and are seldom drawn beyond their own personality. *Narcissism* is the clinical word for this, which comes from Greek Mythology. According to the legend, a handsome young man named Narcissi stopped by a pool of water to drink. When he saw his own reflection he became mesmerized. He remained staring at himself until he eventually died and turned into a flower. Psychiatrists make a lot of money dealing with that problem in human personality. Life becomes all about them, their view, and their experience. Narcissism and isolation feeds upon itself like a disease and it destroys the person's ability to make right decisions. Their emotions become warped, they have no delight in life, and they develop a negative orientation.

Social experiments that have been done document this absolute necessity of a proper relationship with other people. Abraham Lincoln felt that the power that was his as the president of the United States was dangerous. Therefore, he surrounded himself with people who did not agree with him so that having to answer their questions and deal with their opposing viewpoints it gave him proper balance.

I was told of a Frenchman who did an interesting experiment on isolation. He went into Mexico and planned to spend a year in a cave to study how isolation would affect the human personality. He had established food and water in that cave and took a rifle with him so he could survive for a year. He had a telephone, but after two weeks of isolation something began to happen to this man and he refused to answer the telephone. His judgment and his personality became skewed. He was an excellent shot but he could no longer focus and aim his rifle properly. He made friends with a rat. After six months, they had to go and rescue him because he had gone totally bonkers. It proved that the human personality cannot properly survive or function without relationship with other people.

While we were in Israel, there was a woman from Australia in the tour group who had spent time years before living in Israel in a kibbutz. This gave our guide an opportunity to explain the kibbutz movement and how it was instrumental in the settlement of modern day Israel. A kibbutz is basically communal living mostly built up around agriculture. The children were all housed together and only saw their parents on the weekend. This is no longer practiced because they discovered that the children were not developing properly without the parental bond. The book *The Israel Test* by George Gilder confirms this and documents it in detail. This is not the way God created things to be despite what Hillary Clinton believes. It takes a family to raise a child, not a village!

> *But if you have bitter jealousy and strife in your hearts, do not glory and lie against the truth. This is not the wisdom coming down from above, but is earthly, sensual, devilish. For where envying and strife are, there is confusion and every foul deed.*
> *James 3:14-16 MKJV*

James tells us the consequences and the result of isolation. The demoniac of the Gadarenes is another case in point (Luke 8:26-39). This man is living among the tombs, driven there by demons, isolated from society, and cut off from his family. He is naked, howls like a wolf, and in the habit of cutting himself. Jesus brings deliverance and healing to this man, casting out the legion of demons. When Jesus is about to leave the man wanted to follow him, but Jesus tells him something interesting (paraphrased), "I want you to go home to your family I want you to relate to them. I want you to tell them what God has done for you."

Healing in our personalities so we can properly relate to others is part of redemption. Christianity is not, "Jesus and me." When we were in Israel we visited the headwaters of the Jordan River as it comes out of the Sea of Galilee. This is the traditional place for people to be baptized and for many it is the highlight of their life. A whole industry has developed there and many hundreds of people come and stand in line to be baptized in the Jordan River. While there I saw something I have never seen before. There was a group of perhaps fifty people baptizing themselves. They were dressed in baptism robes and everything, but nobody was touching them. As I am watching them putting their hand on their own head and going down into the water, I am wondering, "Who are these people? Don't they trust anybody else to baptize them?" What is this saying about their relationship with God and other people? Even Jesus allowed John to baptize him to fulfill God's will (Mark 3:13-15). Reconciliation with God facilitates reconciliation with your fellow man.

In the film *Epicenter* by Joel Rosenberg, he interviews a Palestinian terrorist whose life had been lived in hatred for Jewish people. But he is converted and the very first thing he does is pray for the peace of Jerusalem. That is phenomenal! Something happens in our personality when we are reconciled to God that makes us want to reconcile with people. The hatred and the bitterness leave and we want favor with our fellow man. I will never forget as a new convert I wanted to give things away. I did not have very much, but this former introvert suddenly wanted to relate to other people. The moment Zaccheus is converted he vows to Jesus to give half of his goods to the poor and pay back fourfold everybody he has ripped off (Luke 19:8). This is a profound revelation of what Jesus Christ can do in the human heart.

Behold, how good and how pleasant it is for brothers to dwell together in unity! Psalms 133:1 MKJV

I had two families come to me one morning after a church service and ask me if I would referee an argument. I told them I did not want to be in the middle of this battle, they should go work it out. One might wonder what kind of pastor am I...just a normal pastor who knows if you are a genuine believer you ought to be able to relate honestly with other people. They did accomplish a truce, are both are in church and love each other. Look at your own faults, bitterness, hatred, prejudice, or whatever has made you isolated from your fellow man. You ought to be able to overcome that as they successfully did. This is the testimony of the New Testament church.

They made it their practice to sell their possessions and goods and to distribute the proceeds to anyone who was in need. They had a single purpose and went to the temple every day. They ate at each other's homes and shared their food with glad and humble hearts. They kept praising God and enjoying the good will of all the people. And every day the Lord was adding to them people who were being saved. Acts 2:45-47 ISV

One of the great blessings that genuine Christian fellowship furnishes is a place for people who are estranged, isolated, and lonely to be drawn together by love for each other. When we dismiss a church service, everybody hangs around. The folks want to be together. I do not know how long they stay because I finally go home, but they are still here. Eventually the ushers have to announce they need to straighten the church up and get ready for the next event. It is a wonderful environment where people who are lonely, isolated, and who desperately need relationship are brought together to relate to one another.

*But I exhort you, brothers, by the name of our Lord
Jesus Christ, that you all speak the same thing and
that there be no divisions among you; but that you be
perfectly joined together in the same mind and in the
same judgment. 1 Corinthians 1:10 MKJV*

The first morning we were in Israel I was passing
out tourist information during breakfast and at the same
time trying to spot those individuals that are in every
group who tend to get lost. If you do not identify them so
you can watch out for them they will be taking a picture
of a rock and the rest of the group will be a mile down
the road. So, I am scanning the crowd and I see a young
man from Massachusetts sitting all by himself. I could tell
he is one of these people who are isolated and does not
easily make friends. I went over to three young men and
said, "Don't look now but over there is a young man, I
want you guys to draw him into relationship because he
doesn't have anybody with him." They went over there
immediately after I had left the table and said, "Hey
come on over here and eat with us." It was interesting to
see that the rest of the tour they all fellowshipped
together. I would say without a shadow of a doubt that
was the greatest thing that happened to that young man
on that tour. God has furnished in redemption the ability
to relate to other people.

Peter failed miserably when he denied the Lord three
times. However, we have this tremendous picture of the
heart of God when the angel of the Lord appears to two
women after Jesus resurrected and says, "*But go tell His
disciples <u>and Peter</u> that He goes before you into Galilee. There
you will see Him, as He said to you* (Mark 16:7 MKJV
emphases added)." This is one of the most profound and
glorious facets in the gospel record because God wanted
Peter drawn back into fellowship. All the disciples knew
what he had done and obviously he is feeling isolated
and unworthy.

Our task is to draw isolated people in to the family of God. The world is filled with people who are isolated in one way or the other and the gospel provides a family that can relate to them and help them have a healthy relationship with God.

Practical Thoughts for Beginning Workers
by Wayman Mitchell

Somewhere we get the idea that, as a pastor, we now function on some spiritual plane where if we just breathe, God will somehow do everything else. The reality is that there are a vast number of things that have a bearing on our ministry and how it affects people.

Buildings

One of the most basic and yet important things in any church is the physical property itself. We all come from different backgrounds, and therefore have different ideas of what is acceptable in building maintenance. In preaching around at some of our churches, I have been astounded by how many people give no thought to lawns, trees, paint, or basic building appearance. In the first church where I was pastor they had dumped debris, junk, partitions, and old broken chairs into the cellar opening which was right at the entrance to the church. This was appalling to me. I have a hang-up on cleaning. Today in Prescott, if I find a wad of paper or any kind of trash, I stop right there and pick it up and take it to the trash can. This is really important and there are many people that will not attend a church just because of the filth. They will come one time to visit, but will be unable to take the disorderliness and will never return. This means that it is vital that the church present an orderly and clean environment.

One of the most important things about the building is the sign. There is nothing that I hate worse than a home-made sign. When a man goes out he has orders not to let his brother-in-law practice his artistic skills, even at half the price, on our property. My orders to him are to go to a professional sign painter, tell him what you want and let him lay it out professionally. People will judge your ministry by your sign. A cheap looking, home-made sign with hand-made lettering on a church building tells you exactly what is going on in there. When I go into a business that looks like a shady operation, then I have no way of knowing what kind of service I am going to get. When you have a good professional sign and building then people know at first glance that you mean business. It is important also to decide the colors you want to use on your sign. Many people do not realize that red and white are the worst colors that you can get. There are many colors that do not catch the eye at all. It has been discovered that people do react to colors. One of the best combinations of colors that you can get for a sign is black and orange. These colors will catch your attention immediately, even in a group of signs.

Just as important is the color of the building. I was pastor of a church at one time with red carpet and blue trim. There is something about red that irritates the human spirit and will affect everything about the service. If you go into a business you can see that they study color schemes; in a fast food place you will see that they use orange and brown. This is because after about thirty minutes they make you uncomfortable. They want you to eat and leave. You say, "The Holy Ghost will overcome all this!" The Holy Ghost is having enough trouble fighting human nature as it is, and if you add to the problems of dealing with people, then you are cutting your own throat. You need to make a study of neutral tones and mild colors that help create an atmosphere in which people are open and receptive.

Lighting is extremely important. All of us at times have functioned with less than ideal situations, but we can do much to help control our environment. Lighting will affect the whole service, so it is vital to get a building that is lit as well as it can be. This is especially true around the pulpit. This will help the speaker to see and the people to focus on him. In Perth, Australia where I was pastor, the building was old and the spotlights shone in the eyes of the congregation as they tried to see the speaker. The first thing I did when I got there was to get a guy on a ladder and have them moved back. It was an irritant and strain that had a bad effect on the people. The first questions I ask of a new pastor when he calls to tie down a building are, "How high is the ceiling; and what kind of lighting does it have?" In a building with a high ceiling you have an airspace that allows people to gather and not be roasted. You put seventy-five people in a building that only has an eight foot ceiling and they are asphyxiated by body heat, and it will tremendously affect your services. It is also a fact that if there is incandescent lighting you will not get enough light and the bulbs will throw off a lot of heat. The only way you can overcome this is to go to the expense of putting in fluorescent lighting. These are the questions that I ask in order to make a decision on a building.

The pulpits in use in many churches are atrocious. When you are young and have twenty-twenty vision you think that it is not important, but for those who are a little more seasoned this is another story. When you start to wear glasses it is much more difficult to read notes. You then need a pulpit of standard height, with a slanting surface that has something on it that is not slick. In many churches you are forced to do a juggling act with your Bible and notes. It is a very simple and inexpensive thing to put construction paper or felt on the pulpit. This will allow you to keep your notes up at the top of the pulpit and allow you to keep eye contact. Eye contact is a very important part of communication, but any preacher worth his salt will preach from notes. If a preacher does not use notes you will not want him back for a second time because he will say the same thing. It is very simple to get a pulpit at a height that allows you to glance down without losing contact with your audience, see your notes and keep the flow going. Attention is kept by eye contact. If a man tries to speak without looking at the audience, he will hold them for six to seven minutes; at which point they will begin to drift off and fall asleep. If you do not believe this, try preaching to one half of your congregation and only keep eye contact with them, then look back to the other side; the people will have drifted off.

Communion

When you go out to pioneer a church, you will pick up some religious folks who are good people. They will come in, put in their tithe and become good workers; they have been looking for something like this. Most of them, before very long, will begin to ask you, "When are we going to have communion?" I was talking to a pastor in Australia about this. Over there, every Sunday is communion time, even in Pentecostal churches. There is no evangelism and no altar call on Sunday morning because that is communion time. That is the way it is; that is the way it has always been; it is an established ritual. I told him, "You'd be wise to have communion before too long. It's not going to make you or break you, and you can have your own convictions about how often it ought to be served. A year from now you can minister your own convictions about it, but for now, it wouldn't be caving in to their religious nature or compromising to serve communion, preach on the blood of Christ, and send them off happy. They won't ask you about it again for six months." It is only wisdom to do that in a new church.

Sunday School

It may not seem important to you, especially if you do not have kids, but most people in America think that Sunday school is the vehicle for training their children. It really is not, of course, but they believe it is. You are not going to overcome in an hour of Sunday school what is learned in the home the rest of the week, but it is valuable. Most people who visit your church will think it is important for their children to have Christian training. They will size up your church on the basis of whether or not you have a Sunday school.

If you have over fifty people in your congregation you should definitely have a Sunday school, because it will do a number of things for your church. First, it will form a basis for visiting families to identify with your church. Second, it will release workers and force them into the word of God, in order to teach whatever age group they are given. This helps them to discipline their minds and, astoundingly, the responsibility will cause them to be more faithful. Third, it gives you responsibility for teaching an adult class. The main reason preachers do not want to have an adult Sunday school is because they already have to prepare three sermons a week and they do not want to add one more. They are lazy. However, the additional study in the different fields that a Bible study will lead you into will bring depth to your preaching and will compute back into stronger, better messages in the months and years to come. Forth, it gives you a platform to deal with problems in your congregation that you could not deal with in a sermon. You will be dealing mostly with the core of the church and you will be able to cover things in a depth and intensity which you could not in a sermon. Fifth, if you are a wise teacher and you allow interaction, it allows you to involve people at their level, and not at the level you think they are. This allows you to ask questions and receive their response, and that brings an uncovering of human nature. You will be astounded at how many people have no idea what you are preaching; if you do not believe this, just ask them some questions next Sunday.

We were involved in a Christmas program on Sunday morning for the toddlers. I was amused to see the unfaithful coming out faithfully. Mom and Dad followed along because their child was in the Christmas program. If you say, "I'm not going to do that," then go ahead and minister to your five people and be happy. However, if you are going to build a large congregation, you must learn to minister to a large diversity of needs. There are people who will never be fully committed to a church, but those people have an influence in the community and witness to people. They will talk about your church, and not harm you, if you will minister to them as they are and hope that someday they will allow God to do as He likes. The wise pastor allows them to become a positive force in the community and does not run them off.

New Convert Class

In the church in Prescott we do this on Sunday mornings during the Sunday school hour. In many churches, they do this on a different night. The problem is that these people are already heavily involved in church activities. When this is done on Sunday morning, several things happen. Instead of doing this yourself, you can allow another ministry to be started. Some pastors feel that their new workers are not qualified, but most pastors are not qualified in the beginning either. Anyone who has been saved six months is able to teach. If they are saved and love your church, they will do fine. Merely use simple materials and help them to answer any questions beyond their ability. This will develop a worker and lay a solid foundation in these new converts.

Overkill

Another great problem in a congregation is a pastor who feels insecure and is trying to establish his throne. He does what I call overkill. This happens when he feels his authority is threatened, or the well being of his future is in danger. Overkill means to take extreme measures in a minor infraction. It is important that we not die on the wrong battlefield.

We had a young pastor years ago in Australia who had a Senator from his area attend the church once or twice a month when he was in town. This young pastor could not appreciate that this man had been saved for a long period of time. He had many interests, and did help the church by his giving and by acting as a Christian influence in that community. The pastor had people give testimonies one service and said, "We only want those that are members of this church to testify." The Senator stood up and the young pastor told him that he was not a member of the church; they did not want him to testify and he must sit down. This devastated the Senator. He was not a psycho or a demon; he was just a man that had something to say. He could not have said anything that was that bad, but this pastor's ego was threatened because this man did not attend every service. This was totally unnecessary and whatever influence the Senator had in that community is now negative. We need to be sure that we are not guilty of this.

I have problems in my congregation, and we will always have problems. As a pastor you move from one mess to another, but that comes with the territory. The tendency many have is to thump the pulpit on Sunday morning and think that you can get these problems all straightened out. So you jump on your white horse with your shining armor and charge. This is the worst mistake that you can make. I deal with issues, of course, but I deal with them in a different way. If I do preach about people's problems, I first get them laughing and then pull out the surgical blade.

I wait until God gives me a green light to minister. People think sometimes that I am ignorant about what is going on, but the fact is there is very little that is going on in the congregation that I do not know about. The "spiritual mafia" will bring it to you. One thing you need to learn is that the facts are not always how they seem. If sister so-and-so comes to you and says thus-and-such has happened, and then you go run off on your horse and preach on that, or go to those people's house and tell them what you have heard, then you are a very immature person. You will find that generally the facts were not right and the situation is not at all like it was told to you. In fact, the person that brought you the information may be the guilty party. If you are not careful you are going to go out and get yourself caught up in a hornet's nest and come out with a bloody nose. There are people problems and doctrinal issues that if you address them from the pulpit it will cause some people to be offended and to become your opponent. People come from different back-grounds and are not always in agreement with all that we do, but I do not mount the pulpit in holy anger. I merely bide my time, waiting for God's opportunity.

In a recent case there was a man who did not believe in tithing. It just so happened that in Sunday school we were looking at giving and worship. I shot holes in his theology, but he could not complain that I was aiming at him because this was a normal part of my study. It worked out fine and he still loves me. In many cases, if you will just have patience, these people will come to you and ask for your advice. Then you can, with tact, address the problem. My responsibility is to try and salvage these people. Do not be involved in overkill. Do not shoot flies with cannon balls.

Prayer Meetings

I am astounded that some of our new churches do not have regular established prayer meetings. I thought everybody in our fellowship knew that this was an important facet of our ministry. I was praying at a regular set time when there was not anyone in our church praying. I have gone to prayer meetings when no one showed, or the only person to come was thirty minutes late. What you are going to have to do is discipline your life! These prayer meetings are a result of your leading and becoming an example. Do not wait for someone to come and say they would like a prayer meeting. This is a part of what we believe. If you are going to have God move, you are going to have to lay hold of God. You need both private and corporate prayer. Establish that you are going to be there praying whether or not anyone else shows up. To accomplish a discipline of prayer in your church, you are going to have to preach on it. When I returned to Prescott from Australia, the prayer meetings had dwindled down to almost nothing. I preached and said, "Folks, tomorrow morning at seven I want to challenge you to join me here in prayer. I want to challenge you to join me one hour before each service in prayer. I will be here and I want you to join me." This caused the prayer meetings to multiply overnight. The discipline that you have in prayer is really important. You are going to have to seek God yourself, and you have to set the example in corporate prayer.

Authority

The real miracle is that people keep coming to your church at all. New pastors waste a lot of time trying to prove that they are God's man of faith and power, and that if you dare cross them you will probably drop dead. In truth, if a pastor will just serve people, they will know who the shepherd is. It is sad that a guy gets a set of credentials and now feels that he has to be called Reverend. A man gets hung up on some title and tells people, "Don't call me Wayman, call me Pastor." I have been called a lot worse things than Wayman and if nobody calls me any worse than that I will be happy. It does not bother me a bit. I do not have to remind people I am the pastor. That is a bunch of garbage and you will not find that in scripture. In fact, you will find the opposite. A pastor is not better than anybody else. You are simply the chairman of that congregation with the responsibility to organize, coordinate, serve, and bring these people to fruition.

Street Preaching

Street preaching is a valid ministry that from time to time all of us are involved in. Every city is different in relation to this. Some cities have places that are especially conducive to outreaches and street preaching. It may be a school, a hamburger stand, or a certain part of the city. When you street preach it has to be with a rhythm. If you allow your people to overdo this in any one place it will destroy your effectiveness. The first outreach will be tremendous, maybe the second and third will be fantastic, but about the fourth time you will get the tomatoes and next the eggs. Beyond that it will turn into nothing but an antagonism session. This is something that has been seen time and time again. You will always have some nut who does not have a platform to speak, and is totally uninhibited. He is in every congregation, and once he gets a group of people standing behind him, he now has a platform. He will do you more harm than good. If you are wise, you will control your street preaching. I am not talking about people witnessing or passing out tracts, but when you stand and address the public, it must be done with rhythm. This simply means that you do it one week and skip the next. This allows you to escape the antagonism.

There are certain places that are made for street preaching. In Perth we had the Hay Street Mall. It is a beautiful place with planters and decorative brick. It is in a large metropolitan area and the street was blocked off at both ends. You could go there and pass out five-thousand fliers before you could even blink an eye. It is one of the best places for an outreach that I have ever seen. The police will even keep an eye on the drunks and perverts and keep them away from you. We had a constant stream of visitors and converts out of that mall, but I know merchants, and if we had overdone it we would have stopped what God was doing. We had one guy in the church that just had to preach there every week. He was one of those fringe lunatics who needed a platform to speak. He wanted to use our covering and go preach. I told him he could go down every Thursday and pass out tracts, but we would only have a street meeting once a month. If you press it too hard, somehow the merchants are going to get an ordinance passed and cut out everything. You may go out in a shopping center and have full liberty right now, but if you turn your nuts loose to put out four tons of literature three times a week, then it is only a matter of time before they get some kind of law to stop you. In some places, young pastors have so antagonized their community that they cannot even have a street meeting anymore. With a little wisdom you can keep a forum for the gospel. Most shopping malls, if overworked, will begin to harass you with security guards and such. Legally, you can go anyplace in America and pass out literature. This has been won in the Supreme Court, and you have a right to do this. In your local area, however, it will cost you several thousand dollars to establish that, and it really is not worth it. Perhaps if you could win forty or fifty souls each time you went out it would be worth your investment of thousands of dollars to win the case. The interesting thing about shopping malls is that they change managers, and if you just wait, it will open again.

We have seen this happen in Prescott. On Halloween we had four nuts dress up like demons and go out to a shopping mall and scare some little kids half to death. We had no idea that this was happening until we got word that an elderly lady nearly had a heart attack after they came up and growled at her and told her she was going to hell. I got a call from the police and had to give orders to the skit team that they were not to go out on the streets without my permission. These are things that your people will do, and they will think they have done a great service to the Kingdom. The merchants rose up and called the police, but we just pulled out. After about a year our people could go there and pass out literature with no hassles. It is really not worth the time and money to fight, so just back off, pray about it, and find another place for outreach.

Praise and Worship

I remember in Australia the folks in our congregation got to where they would do everything but tear the windows out of the building when it was time to praise. When a visiting speaker came up they would whistle, stomp, rattle song books, jump up and down, and give catcalls. In any congregation there will be exhibitionists who cannot relate to or talk to anyone, but in praise they have a wonderful platform where they can express themselves. These are the people who will scream or whistle during the time that we are supposed to be worshipping God. In Prescott we had a woman who used to come to every revival. She was a screamer. We do not want to offend people, and we really do enjoy freedom in the spirit, but this woman would let go with these blood curdling screams. Finally, I made up my mind that I was not going to put up with it any longer. I sat a great big usher on each side of her and told them that when she yelled to put their arms on her shoulder and politely say, "Pastor doesn't want any more of that. If you continue we will throw you out." Sure enough, she manifested, but after they spoke to her there was not another sound out of her. You may think she was having some powerful religious experience, but all this really was her flesh rising up. It is the flesh that wants to draw attention to ourselves; the focus of worship is Jesus. In Australia, with one sermon on the difference between worship and praise, I solved the whole problem. I said that if you want to thank your wife for cooking you a delicious apple pie, try leaning over to her and giving an ear-splitting whistle. That would not go over too good. So why do we come before God to tell Him how much we love and adore Him, and let out a whistle? Scripturally, you will find that this will not hold up. The word for *worship* is literally *worth-ship*. It is giving God our adoration and adulation for who He is. A close word to *praise* is the word *prize*. It is giving to God thanksgiving for what he has done, is doing, and is going to do in the future. Praise is literally vocalizing our appreciation of who God is; His Person and His Majesty as King of Kings.

Some of the extreme manifestations that we get into are counter-productive. As long as you are ministering to a young group of people, it does not really matter. You could do hand springs down the aisle and they would think it was great. As you begin to minister to a larger group of people, though, you will find many who are bothered when people are exhibiting themselves. If you just minister to hippies, the more bizarre you are the more they like it. But if you want to minister to all classes of people, you must realize that there are some things you are not going to be able to do all the time. I am not talking about making your church into a morgue, but laying a scriptural foundation for praise and getting them to worship. You may have elderly people in your congregation. If they have nerve problems, a whistle will absolutely shatter them. It is like putting a knife through their head. If you see them put their hands to their ears, it is not because they are devils who hate praise. It is simply because their ears are in extreme pain.

Lead by Example

As a pastor, you must view your congregation correctly. You will either view them as a field in which to reap, or as a force to which you are called to equip and motivate. If you feel that results happen by your reaping in that assembly, you will act and preach in a way that will handicap revival. Whereas, if you see that congregation as a force that you are going to equip and motivate to go out into the field, your attitude toward those people will be revolutionized. You need to feed the flock more than you correct them. The average pastor feels that it is his job to straighten out his people, so that is the direction of all of his preaching. This is especially true about doctrine. You can go into any congregation and be astounded at what people really believe, but the important thing is that they are effective people who serve God and are soul winners. In the process of time many of them change their doctrine, but they do not change because you convince them. They change because they love you and believe in you. If you believe a certain way then they will also over time if you serve them. You will never straighten anyone out by sitting them down and saying, "You're wrong!" The only way that you will ever change their beliefs is to win them to yourself; and as they believe in you they will become open and change to believe what you believe. If the average pastor finds that someone has a Jehovah's Witness or Mormon background, he feels that he has to mount his white horse and ride in to do battle. This is the worst mistake you can make. You need to pray for those people rather than attack them. It is an astounding thing, but the people whom I become concerned about and begin to pray for, God will bring to me. Then I can deal with them on the basis of their coming to me with a question or for counseling. This opens a door through which I can naturally move in and deal with their need. You have heard it said, "Honey draws more flies than vinegar." You need to begin to trust that through time and prayer, God will change people when your wisdom will not. You may think that you are slick, but I have news for you, only God can change people!

Paul writes, "*My little children, of whom I travail in birth again until Christ be formed in you* (Galatians 4:19 NKJV)." What is he saying? These people had gone astray. He is praying and trusting God to form in them again the right spiritual reference point and posture. You need to learn to do this also.

You need to learn to lead more and drive less. You lead by example. You challenge them to join you. They will not pray just because you preach a fantastic sermon on prayer and yell, "You devils need to begin to pray!" They might nod and say, *Amen*, but they will not do it. They will do what they see you do. People are not good at taking orders at all. We hate taking orders and rebel against it, but we are fantastic imitators. People do what they see others doing joyfully. They will do anything you want them to do if you give them an example. If you want to make them Bible students, preach the word of God. We had a man who came out of another fellowship and he commented that he had never seen a group of men who preached the word of God like the men in our fellowship. The reason is that is the example they have seen; now their disciples imitate them and we have a whole fellowship of men who when you hear them preach, you will hear the word of God. People will do what they see you do. If you want them to be liberal, make sure that when offering time comes that you have something to put in. When there are pledges taken for world evangelism, put your pledge in also. You lead them. They will see that you do not just talk about giving, but you do it. One thing I always try to do, whether I am preaching a revival somewhere or am at home, is to have something in my pocket to give.

Watch your Attitude

All of us struggle at different times with our attitude. We come Wednesday night and the flu has wiped out half of the congregation; or perhaps it is the deer season or the holidays. Whatever the reason, the saints are not there and you had this fantastic sermon to preach, so now you are mad because of low attendance. You get up and begin to harangue those who are there about the *flakes* who did not come. You need to be wise. They never even missed those folks until you mentioned it. But now that you have, they wonder what is wrong and why are people not coming to church. You need to understand human nature. If only half the congregation shows up, you need to say, "Praise God! You folks are a fantastic group! Isn't it tremendous what God is doing? We're thrilled at having you here!" When you point out the problem, you not only defeat yourself; now they feel bad and start wondering if this is a church split or something. You have destroyed the service. If you will just minister what God gave you and have a great service, when the wanderers return people will tell them, "You missed a great sermon!" They will not be able to stay away. You accomplish your purpose, not by haranguing the people who are there about the people who are not, but by blessing those who did show up. The news will spread that you better not miss Wednesday night (or whatever service) because that is where the action is.

Seating

I have noticed a strange phenomenon; people tend to scatter when there is excess seating. This tremendously affects the entire spirit of the church service. In the Prescott Church we had a real need for extra seating because of the conferences. Most of the churches have moveable chairs, but with pews you cannot take them out or close them off. I was worried about that extra seating for when attendance is lower. So, I started turning off the lights in the outside sections and forcing people to sit together in the center. This has revolutionized the song service and affected the retention level of the people.

I read about an experiment done on communication. It confirmed what I had already discovered by accident. In this experiment they had four different settings. There was a large building with people scattered all over; there was one group forced to sit in a small area; there was a house meeting where people were allowed to scatter all over the house, and another where people sat very close, some even had to sit on others' laps. The same speaker presented the same controversial message to all the groups and afterward they gave the people a survey to find the persuasion level. To their astonishment, when the people were forced to come together, they somehow triggered each other to be persuaded. The highest persuasion level of all was when they were crammed into a house. They came to the conclusion that when people are allowed to scatter, they become spectators rather than participate and pay close attention. When brought together, something about human nature and group dynamics cause them to be more easily persuaded, and to affect each other.

You may be too spiritual for this, but for the rest of us, take out the extra chairs in your church. You need to learn to deal with human nature as it is. Use only as many chairs as you need, or even ten less. Stack the extras in the back neatly, and then as the congregation comes in they will be forced to pull together. As visitors come in your ushers can set up other chairs. You will be astounded at what happens to people when they see the ushers putting up extra chairs. It feels like revival. There may not be anyone extra there, but it will appear that way. A person who is excited about what is happening has far greater impact than one who is not. When people are pulled together every aspect of the service, including the altar call, will be dramatically affected by the group dynamics.

Pulpit Mannerisms

From time to time I find a pastor whose ego depends on the response level of the crowd. They will make a statement like, "Jesus is King, amen?" Four people half-heartedly respond, so he screams out, "I said amen?!" People may get in the habit of responding to this, but they will not appreciate it. There is nothing worse than someone in the pulpit trying to intimidate people. There is nothing that upsets me more than to go into a service and find a song leader who thinks he is running some kid's program singing *ring-around-the-roses*. They can harangue me all they want to but I am not about to sing those stupid songs, regardless of what you think. If you want men, then sing men's choruses.

Young ministers have a problem in this area. They try to make people respond. You can push until the people, like robots, parrot back their response, but people who are independent-minded and self-motivated will not put up with this. If you keep pushing and intimidating people, they will find another place to go to church. You are defeating your purpose. Some places I have preached they make you feel like you are the greatest preacher that ever lived. I say things that do not seem great to me, but they will break out in applause. In other places the response level is different. I remember a preacher telling a joke in Australia and the whole assembly just stared at him. It shook him up. He did not know how to handle an audience that did not have the response buttons that he was used to. It is wonderful when people are vocal, but if you are going to measure your success on the response of the people, you are going to be a failure. You need to view your success by what God is doing. I have preached in places where a sermon really got folks moving with me. But then I have preached the same sermon in other places where there was dead silence. I have learned not to judge by the response of the audience. Sometimes the greatest response you get at an altar call (where the real business is done) is with a sermon that you think is a total failure.

Pastors Taking Over a Church

If you take over a church, the greatest asset you have is the former pastor. There are people there who loved him, even if the guy was a scoundrel. You need to give him credit. When people come to you and say, "We really loved so and so," you need to agree and say, "Yes, he did a fantastic job, and I'm going to build on what he's done." Some men feel they have to go in and take the former pastor's name off everything, and change everything that he started. With that subtle undermining you convey the opinion that the other pastor really was not as sharp a guy as they thought. All you are doing is destroying your own credibility. Those people are there because they loved him. He started the church, and it is your job not to say one word against him, or allow a word to be said against him.

When you take over a church, you will soon be approached by those who say, "Brother, we're so glad you're here. We were really having trouble with the former pastor." They begin to fill your ears with garbage. You need to realize that there is a group of dissidents in every church who will put a knife in your back tomorrow. If they will talk against the last pastor, they will talk against you. You are very unwise if you think that now they will appreciate a real man of God. In fact, you are a fool. The people who are the core of that congregation are those who do not say one bad word about the former pastor even though they may know that he had defects. We have one congregation where the pastor is really a strange bird. He is a soul winner though, and those people love him. He makes all kinds of social bloopers. I heard him preach at a conference and my heart hurt for the guy. However, the people love this guy despite his problems because he loves them. Wisdom is to build on what the man who preceded you has done. The average pastor's ego is so threatened that he feels that he is only going to establish his own ministry by destroying the previous man. What he really destroys is himself. The people will not say anything, but in a crunch they will turn against you because you attacked the man they loved and appreciated.

I have a rule that I established years ago. When taking over a church, do not change anything for a year. You may not like everything, but just ride in on the last pastor's coattails. This is not a rule that can never be broken, but it is a general principle that can save you much hurt. After a year has passed, and you have won that congregation to yourself, you can do anything you want to do. I recently had to deal with a problem where the men who were in positions were loyal to the previous pastor. Somehow the new pastor felt that he had to remove all those men and put in men who were loyal to him. The problem is that when you do this you make enemies in that congregation who will do harm down the road.

Choosing Buildings
by Greg Mitchell

Buildings are not the key to revival, but many times I have seen where a man's building was making a hard task even harder. Here are some guidelines in choosing a building for pioneer churches.

Where no counsel is, the people fall: but in the multitude of counselors there is safety. Proverbs 11:14 KJV

Location
Test the waters first before getting a building. This is especially true when pioneering in a large city. The people in one area may not be willing to travel to another area. This may be due to the distance or the danger inherent in an area a building is located in. Because you are new to the city, you may not know the area well and may be unaware of the factors at work. What kinds of people live in that area (demographics: age, race, income, crime, etc.)?

You can test the waters in a given area by having an outreach in a hall, park, hotel, or similar venue. My advice is to do this before you commit yourself to a building! Many men lock themselves into a building lease too quickly without investigating the area. They discover too late that if they knew the area better, they would have decided to avoid that location.

Unless you get a specific word from God about where to locate in a large city, you should look for a building where you get a good response.

Visibility: A critical issue, especially in the beginning stages of a pioneer church, is whether or not people can see the building. Is it easy for people to find the building? As you begin to grow this is not as important because committed people will travel wherever the building is and they will bring others. Americans are very convenience oriented; if it is a hassle to locate or hard to find they are more unlikely to want to come.

If possible, you want to be on a main road where your building is easily identifiable. Put landmarks or some form of identification on your advertising that will help people find it; "Near McDonalds," or, "Across from the pool." Having a suite within a building or one located on the second or third floors makes it harder for people to locate you.

Your building should not be dangerous or spooky. Will people feel like they will get mugged or attacked if they come to your building? That is a good question for you to ask. A simple tip is to look at the building at night! It often looks very different than it does in the daytime. You may discover there is absolutely no traffic or the homeless move into your entryway at night.

Is the building in an incredibly high-crime area where gangs hang out, drug addicts, or prostitutes are turning tricks in the parking lot? If so, then you will only reach that clientele. There are actually some areas that even criminals avoid!

Certain areas have a self-limiting factor. There are areas that are almost entirely made up one people group. It may be an economically depressed area or made up of one ethnic group. If so, typically people from outside that group are unwilling to go there. By locating in an area like this you limit the pool of potential people who will come.

I have heard struggling pioneer pastors bragging about this. They make it a matter of pride that they are in the "biggest, baddest, most dangerous hood in the entire city." They cannot put two and two together...that is why people are not coming!

Paul Stephens has wisely stated, "A good deal in a bad area is death to pioneering!" He knows this from personal experience.

Historically, our churches in America are built on middle-class to lower-middle class people. Wisdom says to find an area like this on the edges of areas you want to reach. In other words, locate in a middle-class to lower-middle class area; reach into the ethnic neighborhood or the economically depressed area, but do not locate entirely in them. It is part of human nature that people are usually willing to move up but not move down. That means that people will usually travel to a better neighborhood, but not to a worse one. It may be a matter of safety or snobbery; regardless, it is a reality you need to factor into pioneering.

Parking: Is there any parking? Is it well-lit? Uncommitted people are usually unwilling to park two blocks away and walk to get to your building, risk their lives, or face danger to come to your event. Parking may be a deal-breaker for the uncommitted.

Appearance

Size: The first mistake we can make is the empty cavern affect. In a new church you do not want your building to be too huge for three people. It is helpful if you can block it off or sub-divide it in some way. The other extreme is the claustrophobic church. If the building is like a large closet, people feel like they have nowhere to hide, suffocated, and anxious.

Signs: The point of a sign is that it be visible. This involves size, position, color, and light. It should be lit at night. It sounds basic, but make sure you check and change the bulbs! For years our concert scene in Prescott was called the Underground because it was hard to see and hard to find. Some nights I would come to the prayer meeting before the concert and discover that either the bulbs were burnt out or the sign had not even been turned on! People are inside praying for visitors to come in from the outside to a building they do not even know is there!

Do not have a hand-drawn or hand-stenciled sign in order to save a few bucks. You are sending visitors a message: "We're the cheesy church, but you can trust us with your life!"

Condition: Your building is often a visitor's first impression of your church. I am amazed at how many men neglect simple maintenance. You might not be able to afford a palace, but at least take care of it! Do not allow your building to be a run-down pit with things broken, the paint peeling, or trash on the floor (Proverbs 24:30-34).

This communicates a poverty spirit that will affect giving. People unconsciously do not have confidence to give to the church that will not spend twenty dollars to fix a small item. There are churches that I have been to where the bathroom does not even have a holder for the toilet paper! A few simple repairs and some paint will go a long way in helping people feel comfortable and confident in the church. I have seen where offerings increased simply by the pastor paying attention to the building condition.

Ceilings: Do not get a building that has eight foot ceilings because it will feel claustrophobic and it will get hot when you get a few people in there. Ceilings that are twenty to thirty feet high are also counter-productive for a beginning church because all the sound will get swallowed up; praise will sound like a BB in a boxcar.

Restrooms: If possible, arrange the sanctuary so that bathrooms are located at the back of the building. It is a distraction to everybody when people walk past the preacher to go to the restroom. Noise from the bathroom (of all kinds!) will distract people also if it is too close to the assembly. If people do not feel privacy going to the restroom in your church they might not come back!

Chairs: Do not be intimidated by the size of your building. Pioneer pastors sometimes set out one-hundred-fifty chairs to fill the space, but they only have three people in attendance. Or, they will spread out the chairs with two feet of space between each, five foot aisles, and forty foot altar space.

It is a scientific fact of crowd dynamics that people listen, retain information, and respond better when they are closer together. Meetings or services have a better feel and generate more enthusiasm that way. It is often better to set out less chairs and have to add more, than have too many and not enough people come to fill them.

Decoration: Men are not so concerned with decoration or the looks of a room so pastors will often let the women decorate the entire building. That is fine, but you have to monitor so it will not come out too feminine. There is a reason you do not find frilly lace curtains, pink paint, and flowery wallpaper in hotels which cater to business travelers. Businesses are decorated to be business-like. Go with the nice but neutral look (unisex).

Negotiating Leases

Deal direct: It is often better to deal directly with an owner rather than a real estate company or leasing agent, if possible. The agents are working on commission so they have an incentive to keep the rent higher. They also are not paying the mortgage each month, so they are less likely to feel the pressure that makes owners more flexible in negotiations.

The length of the lease: Shorter is usually better in the early stages of a pioneer church; one year with an option for more years. A lease legally obligates you to pay even if the church closes down. That means if you sign a five year lease and the church closes down after two years, you still have to pay for the next three years!

Look for hidden costs. Often the lease includes building repairs, maintenance, security, and built in rental increases. I know of a church where the pastor signed a twelve year lease with additional costs and price-increases built-in. That pastor left, but the building was a ball-and-chain burden to that church for years!

Get good advice. Explain clearly all factors to your pastor over the phone. Take pictures and email them. Get an experienced fellowship pastor from the area to come take a look at it.

Where no counsel is, the people fall: but in the multitude of counselors there is safety. Proverbs 11:14 KJV

Outreaches
by Greg Mitchell

Outreach and evangelism is at the center of a successful church. However, it has become obvious to me over the years that many men lack understanding in this area. We need to gain insight into the purpose of outreaches and some practical aspects of a successful outreach.

Therefore those who were scattered went everywhere preaching the word. Acts 8:4 NKJV

The Purpose of Outreaches

This is incredibly basic, but we first need to clearly understand the purpose of an outreach is to create a forum where the Gospel can be presented to sinners so they can be saved! There are three parts to a successful outreach: **forum**...this is either the place or the event; **presentation of the Gospel**...this may involve witnessing or preaching with an altar call; resulting in the third part of an outreach, **salvation**. To help us understand this clearly, we will separate this into two main kinds of outreaches:

First, there is the **spontaneous or unadvertised outreach**. Anywhere there are people the Gospel can be presented! You do not always have to get permission, advertise, or rent a hall. There was a famous bank robber in the nineteen-thirties named Willie Sutton. When asked why he robbed banks, Sutton simply replied, "Because that's where the money is." If you are looking for a good place to have an outreach, go where the sinners are!

So ask the question, "Where do people gather?" They gather in parks, beaches, parking lots, street corners, outdoor malls, and many other places. Many pioneer pastors make the mistake of trying event after event in their building or hall to draw people (often unsuccessfully). Yet, they pass by many crowds of people every day that are wonderful opportunities to present the Gospel through witnessing or preaching! Jesus used a well, a boat, someone's yard, a shopping area, and anywhere else he found people. In the book of Acts they used the temple grounds, a political gathering, and other similar venues.

Another question would be, "Where do people pass by?" Maybe the people are not already gathered, but the location has traffic that could potentially stop or be drawn over to an event. Some options could be a busy street, sidewalk, bus or train station, a school as students are leaving for the day or at lunch time, shopping centers, concerts, or sporting events. There are lots of possibilities, even in smaller communities. We must develop what I call *outreach eyes*. It is the ability to see potential for witnessing, street preaching, or a quick drama. It is keeping an eye out and always being ready for an outreach opportunity.

> *Behold, I say to you, lift up your eyes and look at the fields, for they are already white for harvest. John 4:35 NKJV*

Secondly, there are **advertised or pre-planned outreaches**. In this kind of outreach you do not have an existing crowd; you have to draw them to your venue! The event can be anything that would interest people and bring them to your building, hall, or a park. Perhaps you plan a concert, film, drama, revival, testimony, debate, or children's event. This kind of outreach takes a lot more work. It requires planning, preparation, and advertising. People must hear about your event, be able to find the venue, and have time to arrange attendance.

The Practical Aspects of an Outreach
Pray: Pray for direction. Perhaps God will give you a strategy or a place you had not considered. Pray for help, for God to draw people to the event, and to come into contact with open-hearted people.

One of those who listening was a woman named Lydia...The Lord opened her heart to respond to Paul's message. Acts 16:14 NIV

Ponder: Think about the event! What has worked well here in the past? What has worked well for other guys in the area? What is appropriate for our area, culture, and community? For example, a country and western band in a heavy metal area is probably not the best choice. Showing evolution videos in a very poor or uneducated area probably will not draw!

Prepare: You should be planning and booking your events many weeks or months in advance. In order to get help with impact teams, understand that sending churches do not organize things a week in advance; they plan months ahead of time! Do you need a permit for your event? Some halls or buildings require an insurance rider from your insurer and security guards. Is there an electrical power source, bathrooms, and adequate parking? Make yourself a checklist if necessary. There is nothing more frustrating than having to apologize to a crowd because something went wrong due to poor planning.

Remember, people have lives and schedules. Not everyone is willing to change their whole plan TONIGHT! I used to find it discouraging to hear people say, "I would have loved to come, but I have plans tonight." Maybe with more advanced notice they would come. You do impact teams a great disservice if the only outreach that is done for an event is by them on the day of the event! When showing films as a pioneer pastor I would generally show one film Friday, Saturday, and Sunday nights. Then people would say something like, "I would love to come, but it's bowling on Fridays, we're visiting Grandma on Sunday, but I could come Saturday."

Location: You want the maximum chance at drawing the most people. Is it easy to see? Is it on a main road? Is the location known? Do the locals know the building? Many men make the mistake of going for the cheapest location ("I saved 50 bucks!"), but they sacrifice the number of visitors they potentially could have. It is probably better to pay a little more for a visible location and draw more visitors. Is the location in a dangerous part of town? Especially in larger cities you have to consider this.

Advertising: No one will come if they do not know about it! Our job is to let as many as possible know. If you want a successful event make the advertising look good. I have seen hand drawn flyers that look like they were printed on toilet paper. They were cheap and that was the only message they conveyed. Make sure the invitation has clear directions. Include a map, give directions, or name a local landmark ("Next to McDonald's"). Other forms of advertising you could use would be newspapers, posters in shop windows, banners, radio, public service ads, or television. When advertising for a miracle crusade, know that a picture of the evangelist is not what draws sick people. Use pictures of miracles with captions ("Back injury healed!") Or use names of sicknesses, injuries, or diseases that sick people will identify with. "Hey, I've got that! Maybe God could heal me too!"

Impact teams: Some men never ask for help. One of the greatest resources a young pastor has is the other fellowship churches in his area. Utilizing impact teams can be a great strategy for outreach, not to mention a wonderful blessing to the new converts in your church.

Once you book an impact team, make sure you communicate! If you have to cancel tell them in advance. Give specific details regarding when and where you want them to meet. Also, provide phone numbers in case there is a problem. Give directions and maps of areas you want them to target door to door. Make sure they have clear instructions about what they are to do for the day and what time you want them to meet. Provide refreshments if you can or at least give time for breaks.

Have the team outreach in the area near the event, not twenty miles away! You must have enough flyers for the outreach and prepare your folks to work all day alongside the team. It is always good to have an event that night so the impact team can see some fruit for their labors. Tell the team leaders how many got saved during the outreaches during the day and the event at night. If you are a good host then they will want to come back and labor for you again in the future.

Altar calls: Do not overlook planning for the altar call. You must have convert cards, pens, and people ready to distribute them. Workers must be ready to pray with people at the altar and you need to have folks geared towards ministering to visitors in the altar call. Make sure you collect the convert cards after the event and have the brethren talk to and welcome those who prayed.

When men ignore these basic guidelines, they often come to wrong conclusions. They think crusades, concerts, films, or revivals do not work in their community. You will hear them say things like, "This is a hard city! There are really big devils here!" Maybe the truth is they did not plan or advertise well in the past! The worst thing you can do is give up and stop outreaching.

The Power of Outreaches

While we do believe in advertising, an outreach must be more than passing out pieces of paper with an invitation to an event! Jesus did not invite people to events and he did not use advertising. Jesus challenged people about sin and gave hope for their needs. Many times we fall into the trap of simply promoting an event instead of promoting salvation!

Historically the most likely people to come to our events and respond are those who have already been touched with the Gospel! God works on and blesses seed that has been sown, not flyers that have been handed out!

We have a promise that God's word will have impact on the hearer.

So shall my word be that goeth forth out of my mouth: it shall not return unto me void, but it shall accomplish that which I please, and it shall prosper in the thing whereto I sent it. Isaiah 55:11 KJV

Often the reason why there is such pressure and emphasis put on getting out the flyers is poor planning. There was not enough advance preparation, enough teams, enough outreach before the day of the event. If we planned better then emphasis could be placed on witnessing rather than just getting the flyers out. If we will do our part then God will do his.

I planted, Apollos watered, but God gave the increase. 1 Corinthians 3:6 NKJV

No one can come to Me unless the Father who sent Me draws him... John 6:44a NKJV

For whoever calls on the name of the Lord shall be saved. How then shall they call on Him in whom they have not believed? And how shall they believe in Him of whom they have not heard? And how shall they hear without a preacher? And how shall they preach unless they are sent? ..So then faith comes by hearing, and hearing by the word of God. Romans 10:13-15a, 17 NKJV

Spiritual Atmosphere

by Greg Mitchell

I received a call from a pastor asking my advice about a situation in his church. He told me that every time they get a convert, within two days some religious church will snatch them away. It was not always the same church, and it happened in various ways. His question was, "Can that be witchcraft?" I replied, "Of course, it can be, but the real issue is - what is the source of that?" He told me there was a religious lady in his church who had been coming for six years, and she always challenges what we are doing. She badmouths me, contradicts sermons, voices opposition to discipline, and it seems like every time we get some momentum, she erupts with a new disruption. So my question to him was, "After six years of this, why is she still in the church?" He said he was told to love everybody that comes in the door. So my next question was, "At what point are you going to love the rest of the people by dealing with her?"

This is a very dangerous topic. Pastors who are threatened and insecure will take this to justify chasing off anybody that has a brain. However, it has grieved me over the years to observe men who are pioneering struggle unnecessarily because they fail to balance love with the reality of protecting their congregation.

In this scripture, Jesus goes into a home where a little girl had just died. He wanted to do a miracle for this family and raise her from the dead. But before he could do that, there were some people who needed to leave in order to have a correct spiritual atmosphere. He put these people out and invited certain people in, and then performed one of the greatest miracles in the New Testament.

He was still speaking when someone came from the synagogue-ruler, saying to him, Your daughter is dead, do not trouble the Teacher. But when Jesus heard, He answered Him, saying, Do not fear, only believe and she shall be healed. And coming into the house, He allowed no one to go in, except Peter and James and John, and the father and the mother of the girl. And all were weeping and bewailing her. But He said, Do not weep; she has not died, but sleeps. And they ridiculed, knowing that she was dead. And He put them all out. And He took her by the hand and called, saying, Little girl, arise! And her spirit came again, and she arose immediately. And He commanded that food be given her to eat. Luke 8:49-55 MKJV

The Reality of Atmosphere

Atmosphere is a combination of temperature, humidity, and other similar factors. The reality of life is that atmosphere determines ability. A seed has the potential of life. This is the miracle of God's creation. You can take a seed and plant it, and if there are proper soil conditions and some moisture then life begins to come. But if the elements are not right the seed will not grow. For example, we do not grow bananas in Alaska. There is nothing wrong with the banana seed, but the atmosphere is not correct. Trying that will only produce frustration, and incorrectly concluding that the seeds are duds. This is what happens to many pastors. They come to the wrong conclusion that the seed is no good. They complain, "It doesn't work here. You sent me here. You told me it would work but it does not." The problem is not the seed. The seed's ability to produce is affected by a spiritual atmosphere.

The effectiveness of our prayers is determined by spiritual atmosphere. Daniel prayed for twenty-one days before he received an answer. An angel comes and tells him that he was heard when he first started praying but the Prince of Persia withstood them and so the answer was hindered (Daniel 10:12-13). Do you ever wonder if God hears you? The problem is not that God cannot hear you. Sometimes atmosphere determines whether prayers work.

The Word of God accomplishing what it should has to do with atmosphere. The Bible says, *"He was unable to do many miracles there because of their disbelief* (Matthew 13:58 CEB)." Did Jesus lose the anointing? No. The atmosphere was incorrect.

Atmosphere is most often affected by people. There are many people that are concerned about ruling demons and witchcraft in their area. People will tell you about how big the demons are in their city. I have news for you…they are all big. People talk about the new-age activity in their area. Some people are looking at the evil Satanists. I heard a man preaching who said, "The reason it itches underneath your wedding ring is because the Satanists are praying against your marriage." Just hearing that made me start itching!

Jesus gives us some insight. He said, *"I want Peter, James, and John to be here* (v. 51)." He is saying that these men were going to help the spiritual atmosphere. Then he put out those who were full of unbelief and were hurting the spiritual atmosphere (v. 54). In every church there is a mixture of every kind of person. Jesus said it was like a dragnet bringing in every kind of fish, both good and bad (Matthew 13:47-48). You will never get a church that is one-hundred percent of anything. There will be some that are indifferent, some who are unwilling, and some that are unconvinced. They are not evil; they are just not there yet. The unbelieving can get faith and the unwilling can change their mind. Often when a church gets a new pastor he will yell, "Charge!" He takes off and when he looks back nobody is following. They are not evil; they simply have not made up their mind about the new guy. Serve them, love them, and give them some time and then they will follow.

But this text says, *"They laughed him to scorn* (v. 53 KJV)." This is not doubt; they didn't want Jesus there. We must understand there are those who will actively oppose what we are trying to do. *"And when they saw*

Him, they begged that He would depart out of their borders
(Matthew 8:34 MKJV)."

A church is a living thing that has a spiritual
atmosphere. The atmosphere determines whether or not
the seed works. I have preached in some places where
the word made powerful impact. In other places the
same message will flop because of resistance and
unbelief. In the text, Jesus is going to have church. He
wants to accomplish the will of God. There is death and
he wants to bring life, but before he could, he had to
make some changes.

Poisoning the Atmosphere

You must understand that not everyone who comes
to your church is good. Not everybody who comes to
your church should be there! (This is where we get
dangerous). Have you ever read about Ananias and
Sapphira and thought it was a strange story (Acts 5)?
How do you put that stat on your monthly report? Seven
saved, five baptized, and two killed. Is there anybody
who fully understands that story? I know there are issues
here of money, integrity and honesty, but one simple
lesson is that God is voting dramatically that some
people should not be in church! Here is the truth: Some
people are not brought into church by God, but are sent
there by the devil to influence or change the atmosphere
for bad.

Crazy people

Paul is preaching in a public gathering and there is a
lady who follows them while they evangelize saying,
"These men are the servants of the Most High God (Acts 16:17
MKJV)." She had the right words, but she was screaming
dementedly. You can imagine that those hearing the
message were thinking, "If I go to your church am I
going to end up like her?" The enemy's strategy is to try
and identify crazy people with your ministry in order to
discredit it. I once went and preached for a man who had
first pioneered in a small town with little results. He

thought that if he went to a bigger city it would work out better, but the same pattern was developing. So I went to preach a revival for him and as soon as I walked in I was greeted by this wild eyed man who said to me, "Welcome to The Potter's House!" I assumed he was a psycho visitor, but the pastor informed me that he came every service. A fine looking family came into the service that night and psycho-man went and sat next to them, then asked them for a ride home. I discovered that this was what was happening to every visitor that came. The pastor had been complaining that it did not work where he was, but the truth was that psycho-man was killing his church. The worst part was that the pastor was picking him up for each service.

Religious people

The foundation of a church is very important because it determines what you can build. The people you have at the beginning are very important. This is why the devil will make sure he sends lots of religious people to a pioneer church. I spent years in South Africa as a missionary and it was the most religious place I have been in my life. During an early revival service, as soon as the music started, this man jumped up and did this little helicopter dance all the way down the aisle and around the church. I did not have ushers then, so after church I pulled him to the side and told him to never do that again. He said that the spirit moved him, of course, but I told him it was his flesh and not to ever do that again. The devil wanted visitors to think that is what we do. Men would look at that and think that is what would happen to them if they came to this church. We would actually have visitors come to prayer meetings, women in particular, who would cry out like they were having a sexual experience. I would immediately tell them to stop. The devil wanted to taint our atmosphere with religion.

Immoral people

Foolish is the pastor who hangs on to immoral people because he is afraid of losing numbers. The Bible speaks of a plague that began to break out when the people of God started fornicating (Numbers 25). The lesson is that immorality brings death. In some cases I have seen the favor of God stopped because of immorality in the church. Once it was dealt with, God's favor returned. You will never make disciples in an atmosphere of immorality. It kills the life of God. Phinehas stabbed the fornicating couple through with a spear when they were in the act, and the plague stopped. God promised that Phinehas would be blessed and never lack a man in his family (Numbers 25:11-13). Discipleship is linked to purity.

Rebellious people

There are at least two different categories of rebels. First, there are people who become angry because of discipline. This is a problem in an older church when you have to discipline the children or grand children of long-term members. People do not accept that happily. They will come to church and 'mad dog' you the whole time because you touched their little angel. They are not wicked to the core, they are just upset, and there is hope that God can help them. The second category is those who want to spread false doctrine or dissension, and you cannot allow that to go on.

Very demanding people

The devil sends people to pioneer pastors who will consume large amounts of their time running them ragged. All the energy ends up given to those who are unproductive. A pastor's wife was concerned about her husband who was counseling this lady constantly. She said, "Every time we come to church, if this lady has a funny look on her face then he runs over to ask her about her problem. She will call my husband and ask him to mow the lawn or give her a ride to the store." This pastor was being consumed by somebody he was afraid to lose. Pastors can become consumed by counseling people. You must understand that a pastor's job is to facilitate change; not to change people! There is a difference. Many pastors take this burden upon themselves that they were not meant to bear. People are going to do what they are going to do. If you have counseled somebody ninety-five times and they have not changed, then that should be a clue. Session number ninety-six is probably not going to do the trick. I have been with Pastor Mitchell when he was counseling somebody and he said, "Ok, I have nothing else to say. You have not done what I've told you the last forty-nine times and you aren't going to do it now. There is no point in going on because you don't want to change." That may seem harsh, and I am not advocated being rude, but you cannot let all your effort be consumed by a few so that you have nothing left to give to the majority. A simple question to ask, "If just a few people are able to consume large volumes of your time, then how could you possibly minister if your church was five times larger than it is now?"

The issue is what is released by these various types of people and their effect on the spiritual atmosphere. **The first result is vexation and oppression.** Daniel speaks of a strategy of hell that he will wear out the saints of the Most High (Daniel 7:25). I had a call from a pastor who was describing some circumstances, and I could tell the moment I picked up phone that this man had lost heart. He felt that the situation could not change. This is more than just a bad day, which we all will encounter. The devil can use people as a conduit to bring despair and heaviness. Every pastor is wise to identify who it is that brings heaviness and despair, because you are experiencing a supernatural transfer.

The second result is supernatural resistance. When you have some of these people or elements at work, you will often see a corresponding resistance or lack of results for your prayers and labors. Sometimes you will see the resistance manifest in supernatural ways; "Every time we get a convert, every time we start to get momentum, then some bad thing happens that stops or ruins it."

I want to stress to you the <u>balance</u> to this truth: <u>I do not want you to see every person with any kind of problem as a threat that must be dealt with, or think that throwing people out of church will in and of itself bring revival!</u>

Healing the Atmosphere

First, Jesus got some help. He took Peter, James, and John with him. My suggestion is you talk to your pastor before you take what I have spoken about here and go run people out of your church. A wise Proverb says, "*Be sure you have sound advice before making plans or starting a war* (Proverbs 20:18)." I think many try and get rid of people who God wants to keep and try to keep people God is trying to get rid of. When I was first pioneering, I had a religious couple that came in who believed some odd things, so I spoke to my pastor to get some advice. I was concerned about some great new converts that were in the church. My pastor said to pull the guy aside and make it clear to him that we do not believe like that here. He did not have to believe like me, but I wanted his word that he was not going to spread that doctrine to anyone. So they came for a while, but then he began to publicly contradict me. I assume since he was giving money in the offering he felt the right to express his opinion. I got on the phone to my pastor and described the situation. He said, "Now it is time; he needs to go." I told him I could do it the next service, but my pastor said not to do it in front of everybody because that could be a bad scene where converts could be influenced. Rather, go meet him at work. What a great idea. After he got off work I was waiting for him and I told him, "It's obvious we're going different directions, and since you don't want to hurt the new converts, you need to find a new church." We never saw him again, and he did not do any damage. If I had dealt with it the way I suggested, it would have caused collateral damage publically. Some of those converts are in the ministry today because I got help.

116

Second, you have to deal with the problem. *"Jesus put them all out* (v. 54)." You cannot out wait the devil. Time does not fix things by itself. Time can be your enemy, not your friend. Ground gets harder over time, not softer. Attitudes get entrenched in a congregation over time. Jesus has to make a decision and he is determining the atmosphere. There are a few practical guidelines:

Don't encourage people who are likely to be trouble. In pioneering I had an endless number of people who would show up and say they were looking for a church where their gifts could be used to a greater potential (Hint, hint). They are used to being offered ministry by the religious world. I would just smile and say, "That's nice." I knew they were going to be trouble so why would I want them in my church. In some cases where the person was immediately dripping a religious spirit, I have actually said to people that I did not think this was the place for them.

Do not let trouble people be the center of attention. I had one pastor who had a small building five doors down from a mental health clinic. One of the well meaning members would stand in front of the clinic and invite the patients after they had received their meds. You can imagine the dominant atmosphere that visitors walked into. On top of that, he had this large guy sitting in the very front putting the songs on the overhead projector who was showing his butt-crack. It was ugly. Every person who came in was distracted to say the least. Why would you want this man to be the center of attention?

Sometimes you have to put limits on people. There will be people that you perhaps feel are unclean or dangerous, but you do not have evidence. You can simply give them some boundaries they are not to cross, and explain the consequence is they will be put out of the church if they don't comply. Such as, "I don't want to see you talking to members of the opposite sex," or "I don't want you talking to new converts." Remember that Solomon put limits on Shimei (1 Kings 2:36-37).

You will have to judge those who need judgment. You have to do this carefully. Do not start throwing people out because you do not like them. I am talking about clear-cut violations. If it is not clear-cut, you must use wisdom. But, it must be said, this is a pastoral responsibility! If you are a disciple, it is not your job to do this for your pastor. Jesus did this in our text; he did not get Peter to do it for him.

Finally, Jesus took authority. This is one of the most powerful things a pastor can do. Authority is the right to use delegated power. Jesus took actions and said words based on his authority. He says to the child, *"Little girl, arise (v. 54)!"* He is saying, "It is not going to be like this anymore (death), but it will be like this – there will be life!" Our job is enforcing God's rule and bringing the power of God down to human situations. *"And as ye go, preach, saying, The kingdom of heaven is at hand. Heal the sick, cleanse the lepers, raise the dead, cast out devils...* (Matthew 10:7-10 KJV)."

This is a spiritual posture or attitude that is mostly enforced by prayer. I sometimes will go to the church and pray for people specifically, even laying hands on their chairs. There have been some that I was troubled about, but had no proof. I have had God expose things supernaturally. I have had some that it was obvious they weren't going to stay with us, but I did not want to cause harm to the church. As I prayed, God has removed some surgically – without major collateral damage. But best of all, there have been some that have gotten bent in their spirit, or deceived, but I did not feel that they were evil or needed to leave. As I have cried out to God for them, I have seen many who God touched them supernaturally and opened their eyes so they could get right and recover.

What a joy it must have been for Jesus to see this little girl arise from the dead and be restored to her parents! But remember, the story begins with Jesus dealing with the spiritual atmosphere. That is the potential and the responsibility every pastor has in their own church.

Revelation
by Greg Mitchell

*And coming into the parts of Caesarea Philippi, Jesus
asked His disciples, saying, Who do men say Me to
be, the Son of Man? And they said, Some say, John
the Baptist; some, Elijah; and others, Jeremiah, or one
of the prophets. He said to them, But who do you say
I am? And Simon Peter answered and said, You are
the Christ, the Son of the living God. Jesus answered
and said to him, You are blessed, Simon, son of
Jonah, for flesh and blood did not reveal it to you, but
My Father in Heaven. And I also say to you that you
are Peter, and on this rock I will build My church,
and the gates of hell shall not prevail against it. And
I will give the keys of the kingdom of Heaven to you.
And whatever you may bind on earth shall occur,
having been bound in Heaven, and whatever you
may loose on earth shall occur, having been loosed in
Heaven. Matthew 16:13-19 MKJV*

You may remember the collapse of an apartment
building back in two-thousand-ten in New Delhi, India
that killed sixty-six people and injured one-hundred-
thirty. Upon investigation they discovered that the owner
had cut corners. He used inferior materials, had not dug
deep enough when laying the foundation, and added a
fifth floor when the design was not made to handle it.

It is critical when building a work for God that we
have the proper foundation. This is true for pastors, of
course, but also for anyone who is involved with new
converts in any way. If we build on an incorrect
foundation with faulty materials it will not produce fruit,
last over time, or please God. Jesus is telling us in this
text that the only solid foundation is revelation.

Foundations

How do we build a church? How do we get new people added to the church (not just visit)? In working with converts there are many methods people use to try and get them on track. Some believe the key is information. I have seen people load fresh converts down with everything from Genesis to Revelation before the person even gets up from receiving Christ at the altar. They tell them all the do's and do not's, in's and out's, and who is who in the church. Others think you can pressure or harass people into shape. They are like *Holy Nazis*. If you are not at church they will send the church Gestapo to look for you. If this does not work they put the guilt-trip on people and try to shame them into making right choices. These methods may yield some temporary results, but will not produce life-long followers of Christ.

There have been several cases in the courts of nurses brought to trial for killing those in their care. These caregivers have been nick-named the *Hearse-nurse* or *Angels of Death*. They are supposed to be healing the patients but instead they end up killing them. I have had folks like that in my church. They have a trail of dead corpses behind them as a testament to their methods of working with people. You want to ask them, "What are you doing that is causing every new convert in your care to die?" It is the age-old problem that we can get people saved but cannot get them to lock in. There are churches that have had the same crowd for the last ten years. Other churches do not grow in numbers because even though they get new people, they run the old ones off. I believe God stations angels in front of some churches and when good people come they say, "Not here, they will kill you. Go down the street." They are protecting them from misuse, lack of love, and spiritual death.

Jesus is telling us in this text the true foundation of salvation and the church. In v. 17 he uses the word *revealed*. The word *revelation* means to uncover, to understand, or to get it. People who are unsaved are in darkness, they do not see, or understand. If you are trying to build a church on people who do not have revelation, then you will always be frustrated. Salvation is all about light. Jesus is the light (John 9:5). When people receive Christ they see, they understand, they get it. You cannot trick people into getting saved. You cannot impress people into getting saved. The only way somebody gets saved and stays saved is by seeing their sin as God sees it and seeing the work of God through Jesus Christ. Peter says, "*You are the Christ* (v. 16)." This is revelation! Anything less will not produce fruit or last over time.

If revelation is the key, then whose job is it to bring revelation? That is the critical question if you want to be affective in working with people. Revelation is a miracle that only God can bring. Jesus tells Peter, "*Flesh and blood did not reveal this to you* (v. 17)." You cannot harass, pressure, guilt, or inform somebody enough to accomplish this. The Father in heaven brings revelation. It is not your job to change people! There are pastors who are frustrated, banging their head against the wall because they are trying to make people get it. I have tried all of the wrong ways to get people serving God. I thought if I could get them in a head lock, twist their arm behind their back, or threaten them; none of it works. Revelation is a miracle! People have to see it in order to do it. If they are not seeing it, then nothing you can do is going to change them.

Differences

This scripture shows us that there are differences in revelation. When you deal with people you have to understand that not everybody is the same. People will not get it at the same time, in the same way, or to the same degree. In the text he is asking twelve men the same question, "*Who do you say I am* (v. 15)?" Only one of them gives the correct answer. The other eleven do not get it yet and that is okay. We are not kicking them out or giving up on them because they are not catching on.

Everyone operates at different speeds and levels. If you do not understand that you will be frustrated in working with people.

Jesus spoke to different people differently? He spoke to the seventy differently than he did to the multitudes. There were things he told them that he did not share with the crowds of people that gathered. He told the twelve things that he did not tell the seventy. There were things he told the three disciples that he did not tell the twelve. Why? People are different. Success in working with people depends on working with them on the level of their revelation. You have to have room in your heart to let people function at their level. Some people can take it straight and heavy, but others need it gentle.

But we were gentle among you, just as a nursing mother cherishes her own children. So, affectionately longing for you, we were well pleased to impart to you not only the gospel of God, but also our own lives, because you had become dear to us. 1Thessalonians 2:7-8 NKJV

There is a woman named Carol in the church in Perth, West Australia who is a legend among the churches there. The Sunday morning Carol came to church and received Christ was a sermon on fasting. That is unique in itself. At the conclusion of the service the pastor challenged the congregation to a three-day fast and Carol raised her hand in commitment. For the first three days of her salvation she fasted and was in prayer every day. Thursday, the day after the fast, she was on outreach and telling people about Jesus. That next Sunday, she started tithing. Carol is a legend because that is so rare. I wish every convert caught on that fast, but if that is your expectation you are going to be extremely disappointed. You must have the ability to allow people to function at their level.

I have spoken to men who boast that their congregation is a dedicated, green beret, delta force for

Jesus. Some think that is the only way a church should operate. Men will point out that they have one-hundred percent attendance at every prayer meeting and outreach. I am not impressed by that. Why? Not because I do not want people to pray and go on outreach, but because I realize ministries could grow so much if they would just open their heart to less committed people. I know that sounds like heresy to some. I have heard men wear it like a badge of honor, "We are a small but committed church." I had a man tell me one time, "This couple we are working with obviously is not serious about serving God. Just because their sick grandmother is visiting from overseas they are not going to come to church tonight; can you believe that?"

There are two types of people that are deadly on new converts: First, those who caught on immediately upon conversion. They expect that from everybody, "What do you mean you are struggling with sin? When I got saved I left everything!" Secondly is somebody who was saved in an atmosphere of absolute revival where the growth rate was off the charts. The church in Perth was like that. The first pastor smoked, but the church still exploded in growth (It is not good that the pastor smokes! Do not make a church growth doctrine out of that. The point is that there was a grace and the church was growing regardless). The problem is that people who are saved in that atmosphere then go to a city to pioneer and think that they can treat people however they want and still build a church.

You cannot move people beyond their level of revelation. This involves timing. In our text, Jesus has been with the disciples for three years, yet is just now telling them about the cross. Many workers are frustrated because they are moving ahead of the people they are trying to minister to; trying to take the person where they are not yet ready to go. In fact, you can kill people if you give them too much, too fast. I read about a fifty-four year old woman in New York arrested for criminally negligent homicide because she gave her daughter an adult dose of prescription pain medicine and it killed her. If your head hurts, a painkiller is good. However, do not give an adult dose to a child who cannot handle it yet. It is not the patient's fault they are dying when in fact they were not ready for what you were giving them.

When I first pioneered I had some biker chicks that got saved and were on fire for God. They brought their husbands but the men were a little slower in getting it. They came to church but were limping along. I wanted to open up the Bible with these men, pull out the concordance, and make them disciples. What they wanted to do was play tennis. So, I played tennis. That was there level. Later on they began to make decisions about alcohol, take stands, evangelize, and give. But that took timing. If I had jammed them in the first week I would have killed them all. You have to allow for progression in revelation.

For precept must be upon precept, precept upon precept, Line upon line, line upon line, Here a little, there a little. Isaiah 28:10 NKJV

Some workers are impatient and do not want to wait. Why the hurry? They feel God is taking too long and so they want to help Him out. It might be their ego on the line. These slow pokes are making them look bad. We want to give a positive report when the pastor asks, "Where is that person you are working with?" If you are pioneering and your pastor is coming to preach, you do not want to have to make excuse for missing or struggling people. That is why we resort to the pressure method. We demand people shape up because we want our pastor to commend us. Pride is the motivation, not honoring Jesus or care for the people.

Confidence

The location of the text is Caesarea Philippi. The city is built on a huge rock and the major false religions of the day had temples there. There is a natural spring in a large cave which was believed by the pagan worshipers to be the gates of hell. Part of the rituals to entice the gods to come up from the underworld through this gate included prostitution and sexual relations with goats. Jesus deliberately takes his disciples to this place of human depravity. Why? It is human nature to think that people are never going to change. Many men consider their city to be worse than others; "More witchcraft per square inch than anywhere in America." Jesus brings his disciples to the capital of witchcraft, idolatry, and perversion. He does not ask, "Who are these people?" But he asks, "Who am I?" The issue is not how big the devils are; devils are devils. The key factor is who Jesus is! God is greater than witchcraft, perversion, idolatry, and any human problem. If you are going to build a work for God you have to have confidence that God is able.

Only god can reach into a human heart and change them. We had a couple that came to church for a few weeks then faded away. Over the last few years they would appear again, come for a couple of weeks and then disappear. Just recently the wife showed up and answered the altar call. Her husband was in drug rehab, so she came by herself for several weeks. When he got out of rehab he came and said, "Whatever you did to her while I was in rehab I want you to do that to me. She is a different woman." That is revelation; she really got it because the Father revealed it to her.

If it is God's job to bring revelation, what is our responsibility? First, we must contend for revelation. We trigger that by prayer (Ephesians 1:17-18). That is our job. Second, we must be trustworthy with the people God gives us. Not all the converts we get are good converts. Some will frustrate you to no end. God wants to know if He can trust you with good people.

Not long after my wife and I got married we made a commitment to the will of God for our lives. We began to throw ourselves into the visitation ministry. We tried our best. We had liars (they did not live at address given), immoral people, religious people, and people who have no category at all. It was frustrating. Then one day my wife prayed with somebody at the altar and we took her out to eat. She said at lunch, "Hey, can I come to church tonight as well?" I almost choked on my food. We were use to people not wanting to come. That evening she asked, "Am I allowed to go with you on outreach?" She had revelation. God had watched us try our best with all the hard cases to see if he could trust us.

His lord said to him, Well done, good and faithful servant; you have been faithful over a few things, I will make you ruler over many things. Enter into the joy of your lord. Matthew 25:23 NKJV

There was a long distance trucker who got saved in Perth, Australia back in nineteen-eighty-four. He lived on the other side of the country in Melbourne; we were planting a couple there and so he locked into that congregation. In the process of time I took over that church as pastor. He was a great guy with a great personality and I loved spending time with him. However, he was lazy and would frustrate me because I could see the potential in him. I could not make him change; the only thing I could do was love him, and work with him at his level. Years later I was speaking with his pastor and asking who was going to get sent out at the upcoming conference. He tells me he is going to launch this man and his wife. I was shocked. He had frustrated every pastor he had for twenty years. What happened? Flesh and blood did not reveal this to him. The Father in heaven changed him and now he is a missionary in India. Not long ago I went and preached for him and God is using him powerfully. How many men like that have been run off or given up on because we did not have enough patience, trust in God, or would not let go of our ego? They could have been someday great; the Father could have given revelation. Jesus said, "*I will build My church, and the gates of hell shall not prevail against it. And I will give the keys of the kingdom of Heaven to you. And whatever you may bind on earth shall occur, having been bound in Heaven, and whatever you may loose on earth shall occur, having been loosed in Heaven* (v. 18-19)."

A Conversation with Pastors Wayman and Greg Mitchell

How did the vision for planting churches get started? Did you have a vision of this before it happened or did you "walk into it?"

W. Mitchell: Well, it had to do with the time frame, when God was touching these young hippies who were traveling coast to coast, uprooted, and rebellious, doing drugs, and immoral. I came here to Prescott and in the first church service there were twenty-nine people including my family of seven (January 11, 1970). We had a revival with John Metzler and God touched a young couple who got locked into our church. God moved through them and they started bringing in some of their friends and they started getting saved. So out of that began revival, but there was no vision that I had, like this great plan. It was something God was doing in a time frame of touching these young hippies that were open to God and so it was just a spontaneous thing. As more people got saved and we started reaching them, then we had a burden to reach out beyond our own walls and so it was a thing that grew, it was no great revelation that I had.

What would you emphasize in a book on pioneering?

W. Mitchell: Well, get the gospel outside the four walls is the main thing. You have to understand the mindset of the Christian world is you get people to come to your facility and that way you can influence them. But the thing that we emphasize, which we began in the early days, is to get outside the four walls where the sinners are. Music was a the big scene then, and we got musicians saved who wanted to express themselves and so we started doing outreach and concerts and we drew sinners to those concerts. So outside the four walls is the concept for pioneering. If a pioneer pastor goes somewhere and they just hang a sign up and expect people to come they are going to fail. They've got to find some method to get the gospel outside; door knocking, street preaching, concerts, or whatever, it's got to be outside the four walls.

Did you start with basically the same support concepts as are in practice today, or has that also developed over time?

W. Mitchell: That came out of my own experience when I was in a denomination. They were fully willing for you to go somewhere, but if you go, you are on your own. The concept of support was not done, period. So it was out of understanding that there needed to be some support for people to go and do a work for God. That is why we began to send workers out and why we began to support them.

G. Mitchell: *The concept of support is a privilege. It allows somebody to fulfill their calling. Some guys begin to see that like an employee and complain that we are not paying them enough money. It should stir gratitude for the mother church and a sense of obligation to build according to the pattern and not do your own thing.*

W. Mitchell: It is very rare that anybody would invest like that in another.

Do you still send out men on full support?

W. Mitchell: That depends on the person. If they are a new pastor, we will give ninety days' support, and we reevaluate it from there. If they are doing well and have promise we quite frequently carry them longer. If it's a seasoned worker then that is a totally different scene. For instance, we recently pioneered a city with a man who came back from overseas. He is seasoned now and we fully supported him. I just got his report and he is running sixty something people. We cut his support down now because he's making good impact. So it depends on the person.

What do you tell a young man just before he goes out to start a church? What kind of things would you emphasize to him in the very beginning before launching him out?

W. Mitchell: Historically, I have emphasized that they have to hit the ground running. Immediately they need to find a venue of some kind where they can do something; a club house, community center, apartment complex, motel, or conference room. Because the danger is to lose impetus, get diverted and lose the excitement of the thrust... so hit the ground running. Hold Bible studies in your house, in your apartment, do something. **Get started right away, do something right away. Don't wait six months before the perfect building comes along?** Absolutely! Don't go into a city and call the next week and say, "Hey there is this building I can get..." because you don't know where the people are going to come from. Men go in trying to get a building right away and then when they outreach all the people come from different areas and then they want to move...**but now they are locked into a lease.** Exactly!

What are some foundational things that a pioneer pastor needs to establish at the very beginning in his church?

W. Mitchell: The problem is too-soon-itis. They want to preach strong meat sermons that they heard in the mother church. My advice is giving them happy juice at first. You have to make them Christians before you make them disciples so don't try to come on too strong. The main thing is to get them saved and filled with the Holy Spirit; get them involved in outreach and ministry.

Can just anyone go and start a church?

W. Mitchell: Well, of course not, there has to be some adaptability. The main issue is people skills, which is why we have discipleship and we give men some experience with people. Building a church is actually getting people to follow you as you follow Christ. Paul said, *"Be ye followers of me, even as I also am of Christ* (1 Corinthians 11:1 KJV)." You have to convince people that you know where you are going and want to help them.

Can you make a man a preacher?

W. Mitchell: You can't make a man a preacher but you can hone some of the natural skills that he has if he's called. Calling is something that God does that we recognize, reinforce, and facilitate, but as far as making a man a preacher, I don't know how we can do that.

How would you identify the call?

W. Mitchell: Well, you can recognize the burden a person has, how they conduct themselves, and their dedication. From time to time somebody will ask, "Can you tell me whether I am called or not?" That is not my place; you must talk to God about that. However, we can recognize some of the signs are burden, dedication, Bible study, being involved in ministry, outreach, evangelism, witnessing, and so on...**and fruitfulness?** Yes.

Do most men seem to wrestle at some point with their call?

W. Mitchell: I am sure they do, I know I have. Something happens...you are absolutely positive that you are called but then slow times come and you wonder if you are called. **So guys vacillate...and there are guys who say they are called who are not and those who say they are not called, yet you know they are...?** The old cliché says, "How eager is he whom God never sent, how slow and hesitant is his chosen instrument." I had a guy years ago that said to me, "Pastor, God's revealed to me, I got this revelation from God and he said you are going to put me in the Tucson church as pastor." This guy was not even qualified to be a Bible study leader; he was delusional.

G. Mitchell: *That is the beauty of discipleship. In the process of time there is a natural weeding out process. Those who say they are called but don't have the skills, time reveals it.*

If it was only x-number of class credits that qualified a person, they could hide their true character. But through the nuts and bolts process of discipleship, relational skills and calling is demonstrated. Ultimately, calling can be seen by others. It begins within a man, but at some point it is recognized by others. There should never be a reaction of shock when somebody is placed in ministry (except from those who have a problem with jealousy).

W. Mitchell: *"Therefore, brothers, pick out from among you seven men of good repute* (Acts 6:3 ESV)." This is peer recognition. **It would be nice if all that would be revealed in the mother church, but sometimes you invest a lot of money in a man to find out down the road that...** So, as Greg said, time plays it out.

Is there a mystery in church planting and ministry?

W. Mitchell: The mystery is why some guys make it and some guys don't. There is another mystery: that you can put a man in one place and he does absolutely nothing or very little, then he shifts into another city and it explodes. If we could solve that problem we would do nothing but have success.

G. Mitchell: *And then you have the reverse of course: the man who you think is an absolute winner and he does zilch.*

W. Mitchell: This is God's work and you have to touch God and find out what he is saying. The church is not an organization and this is what bugs us...if it was like an Amway program then we could organize this correctly and say the right things and put money in this or that and know it's going to succeed. But it's not like that. Many churches are nothing more than a business; nothing more than a social network sorority or fraternity which will naturally produce a group of people but are not going anywhere supernaturally. In a business model you have business principles, you organize people and produce a product, and some people will be attracted. But that is not what we are doing. We are attempting to change souls and get them saved. We have a brand new convert who just got out of prison after seven years...for

133

him to be attracted to church is a miracle. That is supernatural. Last month we baptized three men fresh from prison; the one who was in seven years, a guy in two and a half years, and another one Sunday night who was in fifteen years. This is red neck city, Prescott, Arizona; this is God that has drawn these people. Apparently we have something that can help them. The Lord is moving; that has to be the factor behind it all. God has to do a work. This is how we got to where we are: God was doing something and we simply stepped into it. For instance, the coffee house ministry is what God was doing. I am not musical, I wouldn't recognize a pot plant if I saw one, but something in me resonated with these young people and it drew them. They knew it was a place they could get help. Why Prescott Arizona? This is a great mystery; with population back then of only thirteen-thousand-five-hundred people. It wasn't that I had this great vision; it was God doing something that we tied into and flowed with. There were coffee house ministries all over the world that went belly up. I went to Phoenix in the early days and the Paradise Valley Baptist Church had tied into this. There were probably thirty-five-hundred people gathered. Outside the church were cars parked up and down the road, you couldn't even find a place to park. But they didn't capitalize on that and take it in the right direction. They finally wound up in downtown Phoenix, old Church of Christ building, and today it's totally gone. We are still functioning in ministry and it has to be because we were able to solidify some of these converts through discipleship and perpetuate the movement through church planting.

Discipleship and church planting is that what you refer to as the pattern?

W. Mitchell: Yea, it is a pattern that we stumbled into though and not some vision; we just simply wanted to reach souls and they were getting saved. We first got into this by sending music groups out (to surrounding communities) like Eden and Living Waters to do concerts on Saturdays and a lot of people were getting saved. We tried to put them into local churches but the fruit was being lost; that is how we got into church planting. So we had to plant churches ourselves to retain these converts. Our first church was in Wickenburg, AZ, a town of fifteen-hundred people in the summertime and twenty-five-hundred in wintertime. We planted a rock musician in a cowboy town and in seven months he was self supporting. And so we continued on from there. The real issue was that out of church planting and discipleship we were discovering the dignity of the local church. In the local church are all the ingredients to evangelize and reach out to regions beyond. This is not a denomination thing because in the church world they have a national evangelism office and church planting office where you send money. Church planting should be a local church function for a bunch of reasons that are tied into this one: they plant one of their own that is raised up and that the people identify. Two things happen out of that; one is that they give to send that person because they know them and they have a local identity. In a national program they give ten dollars, but if it's one of their own they give hundreds. They will pray for him and go on impact teams to help him because they know him. The second thing is within that church they see one of their own that is raised up. They say, "I know this guy and if he can make it maybe I can make it." See many people don't recognize that element but it is one of the dynamics that flows in our fellowship.

Is pioneering critical to the church and to the life of the church?
W. Mitchell: Absolutely. **Every church needs to strive to make disciples and plant churches?** Yes, that needs to be their goal to plant their first church. We are reaching the world, so it's absolutely essential for the local church, but not before they have the strength to support. Otherwise they stifle the worker as he goes out; he's got no help, he's got no money for a building and so

he says this doesn't work. It does work but it has to work within the framework of the reality.

How important is pioneering to our fellowship to continue life and continue growth 40 years later?

W. Mitchell: It's absolutely essential because without it a number of things happen: one is the church stagnates locally because there is no vision. The only vision that they have is to buy new carpet or to get some new equipment or to do some local activity. When there is church planting it increases an excitement that nothing else can.

G. Mitchell: Also, without pioneering there is no vision for other disciples to follow. Disciples see their own brother, their own friend who gets planted out, they see the transformation in what he is becoming and that is what makes an impact. Disciples remark to me, "Pastor, I can't believe it when I listen to this guy preach and look at him working with disciples." That gives them the desire to want to follow and without that discipleship would go down. Without pioneering you have no perpetuation; it's not a program, but the vision perpetuated by pioneering.

W. Mitchell: It's a spiritual dynamic that is a work, it's not catalog. Last night at a pioneer rally this young man I've seen over the years who is now a pastor was taking the offering. I am listening to him…here is this little kid, I mean he is mature and did a very good presentation for the offering. You would think he's been a pastor for 20 years and so that is what Greg is talking about. Anybody who knows him can see the development in this guy and be very encouraged in what God can do in the process of time.

G. Mitchell: You would never get that in a denomination where we are just giving to a program somewhere. Men see the possibilities of what they can become and they aspire to that.

Must a pastor strive to keep that alive in his church?

W. Mitchell: Stagnation can set in when a pastor becomes comfortable: now they have money in the bank and they have a congregation to preach to; or perhaps they've had a few bad experiences like one of their guys on the field rips off a church. Now he says, "Hey, I need to calm down here." So they begin to manage what God has put in their hands and they don't want to risk anything. See, church planting is a risk; discipleship is a risk. When you put it into the hands of a disciple to conclude an outreach, for instance, like we do in the plaza, it is a risk. Here is your investment, here is potential fruit and you trust it to a disciple. It is a risk because they could fail, and sometimes they do. I've never preached an outreach except for the Fourth of July God and Country celebration. We did an outreach years ago and the guy who gave the alter call...you'd think he was selling used cars, "Christians have fun too." I could have killed the guy! I wanted to walk on the stage and strangle him. There were fifty to sixty visitors in there. So it's a risk and pastors don't always want to invest the time, the effort, and the money and then have a failure. The ego is also involved: you put your hand on this guy and you send him out and he's a blooper; it reflects on you...and so they would rather settle in and become managers. Discipleship comes from a sincere desire to help another fulfill his destiny. If it is about your ego then you will not be involved in discipleship. You won't let disciples pull an altar call because they may screw up and make you look bad.

G. Mitchell: *It just boils down to hard work over the long haul. It is very common in our fellowship that men do get excited to plant their first church. But then the problem is the ongoing. You are going to be doing this...we are going to be doing this until we die and that is the real issue. It's the hard work of discipleship: you get a disciple, finally work out the kinks and get him functioning the way you want him to, and then you launch him out. Then you start the process all over again. The problem is it becomes wearying: all the factors of the failures, the rip-offs, the disappointments, and your ego...all that plus the ridiculously hard work. Many pastors would rather pull back and not make it so hard for themselves.*

W. Mitchell: And it is expensive, as Paul said in Philippians *"you sent aid once and again for my necessities* (Philippians 4:16 NKJV)." There is the reality of continued support.

G. Mitchell: And so you have to be totally committed to the vision; not as a program but as a passion. If you don't have a passion it won't continue long-term.

You have used a term often that seems to be important to our fellowship, "the indigenous church," how does that relate to the objectives for the pioneer church?

W. Mitchell: We are talking about a church that becomes self-supporting. It is self-propagating because you don't have to watch over it and keep it alive; it is self-governing in that they put the same disciplines and standards in place that the fellowship believes. Our aim right from the beginning in foreign countries is an indigenous church. This does not mean that they are independent, but that they repeat the same things that we have done: they plant churches, they put the same standards in place and they propagate themselves within the country. And that has been very successful in other nations.

Does the pattern alter because of culture?

W. Mitchell: Obviously, it has an effect. You have a local flavor to it that has to fit in with local culture and adapt to it, but you must beware of losing the basic principles because it's a biblical pattern. We have only tried to repeat the biblical pattern. When I came to Prescott years ago an evangelist gave me a word from the book of Isaiah and said that my ministry would be restoring the foundations and that is what it has been. What we are doing isn't any different from what the Bible teaches. In the New Testament church this is what they did, *"And daily in the temple, and in every house, they did not cease teaching and preaching Jesus as the Christ* (Acts 5:42 NKJV)." I was asked earlier this week about the practice of knocking on doors...It's just one way outside the four walls. Is it fantastically successful? No! Nothing you do is fantastically successful. It's like street preaching…do you get 40 people added to your church? No! But it's a spiritual dynamic that gives boldness to your people and establishes spiritual dominion in the city. Anything that gets the gospel outside the four walls; a park outreach, concert, or whatever, just get outside the four walls…that is the principle. In doing a crusade, for instance, I won't go inside a church and do a crusade because you don't have the dynamics and I ask where it is before I even accept an invitation.

You have seen a lot of churches begin. As an overview, what would be three things that cause men problems?

W. Mitchell: One is they try to build with religious people and as a result of that they put people into positions that have not been saved in their church. Second thing is that they are trying to make disciples before they make them Christians. Then a third would be the money factor: they sometimes don't want to preach on money and put a responsibility on them and so there is an improper development there.

G. Mitchell: *Another would be people skills. They don't have them. We talked about calling and guys who go out, don't do well and their conclusion is they are not called. Obviously, that is between them and God but I think the real factor is many times they are called but they absolutely lack people skills and do not possess the flexibility to change that. So they negate what God wants them to do. So lack of people skills would be a huge factor.*

W. Mitchell: They don't know how to help people in crisis. Not everybody that causes you problems has to die. It's the old saying, "butchers and surgeons, both of them cut but the outcome is far different." This is not something you can put on a diagram, but when you are dealing with people you have to be sensitive to how far you can go in trying to bring correction, repentance, and healing to them. For many men it's, "You don't like it, then outta here." Sometimes that needs to be done but that is not the norm. Guys will justify small crowds by saying to you, "Man, we got real Christians." You have to be able to keep people coming long enough to get help instead of saying, "You're outta here."

G. Mitchell: *"Treasure in earthen vessels" (2 Corinthians 4:7) means that the gospel cannot be separated from man. This means character, but it is also personality. The ability to connect with people is one of the things that you find in a successful pastor. Invariably, the people who struggle the most are the ones who do not understand this. They think it's all up to God, but you have to make people like you because they don't understand Jesus yet. You have a man who is stiff, brittle, or obnoxious and they do not have the ability to make people like them. Why would I want to come back to his church when this guy makes me uncomfortable? I preached in Russia a sermon on people skills that struck a chord with them because they are having great success with drug rehabs. The problem is in drug rehab they totally regulate their life. If you do not pray, if you do not read your Bible, if you do not come to church, and go out on outreach then we kick you out. So, that's handy in a drug rehab but the problem is when these converts come to church they want everybody to be like that and they end up running people off.*

What are some other marks of men who do succeed? Are there any other character traits or things they do that seem to identify them?

W. Mitchell: Well, they apply themselves to the Bible. You are not going to be successful just simply standing up and giving some kind of lecture or some kind of talk. The Holy Spirit will only confirm the word of God, not your joke or illustration. So they must have knowledge of the Bible and cultivate that and enable that to grow because your major task is feeding people something that causes them spiritual health. That is the responsibility of the man; you can't do that for him. They are going to have to have a spiritual dimension and that is only gained by personal dedication and prayer. A person who does not engage the Holy Spirit in prayer is not likely to have a spiritual dimension that is going to do a super natural thing in people. This goes with people skills also because it's a spiritual dimension in your life that enables you to measure people for what you can and can't do with them. It's like a dance, there has to be a rhythm and an orchestration with a spiritual dimension and sometimes you can say things to people that at other times you can't say. It has to be in the right timing and that only comes by supernatural ability from the Holy Spirit. You are not going to have that if you are just simply filling an office or position. So, it is essential that a man surrenders to the will of God. Sometimes you offer an opportunity to a man and he declines because, "It's too hot there, I can't go to a desert area." This is the same man that has never been successful though he's been in several different places. It's really about the will. We often remark on this: thirty years ago you'd say to a man, "Listen, I want to talk to you about an opportunity..." And he says, "Yes, I'll take it!" You haven't even told him where it is yet! But today they want to know, "Do they have a medical program there?" We offered a guy a church sometime ago and he said, "I can't do that now because the State is furnishing braces for my kid's teeth and if I move they would lose that." Men have all these little things they require these days. So, it's the will that needs to be surrendered to God. Often that is discovered when leadership offers you an opportunity. It doesn't come on a big screen and say, "This is the will of God." It is essential to surrender to the will of God and to trust headship to measure an opportunity. One of the things that anybody who knows me will say is that I do not make people go anywhere. I offer an opportunity and they say, "I don't feel good about that," or, "Yes, I will do that." I take that as God helping me to not miss the will of God in an opportunity or a person.

What would happen if you forced a man into a location?

W. Mitchell: If they did not succeed you would be blamed, "You ruined my life, you made me do this." We've had guys that said, "I am not successful, my marriage failed because you wouldn't send me out until I was married and so I married this chick and she's the wrong one." Or, "These people here are not responsive to the gospel and so you made me come here and that is why I failed. It was the wrong city."

How did you know you were called to come to Prescott?

W. Mitchell: Well, I didn't. This is my hometown and so at one time I wanted to come here. It was a fairly successful church of a hundred-fifty people or so and there was a pastor change but they wouldn't offer it to me then. It wasn't until they had a total moral failure here (the pastor and his son both ran off with women in the church), that is when they called me and offered it to me. My first response was, "Oh now you want me to have it!" But the real fact was that I had become disillusioned with the organization because I saw the politics. You have to understand that in the denominational world you are waiting for promotion to a better church and so that is your mindset. I had taken a church and split it. I had revival services with Johnny Metzler and the old saints rose up and three families left. I was in Carson, California and it was a bad scene. I had taken that church and after I was there a week seven women came and told me they were credentialed to preach and fully expected me to give them the opportunity. I told my wife, "We can build a church here but I have to run those people off." So then it dawned on me that this is what I am dealing with and it didn't matter what church I took. If I took the things that I believe in like preaching biblical standards, then I'm going to split that church. So I was disillusioned at that point in my life. I just wanted to have a church where I could have a place to live, preach, and I could raise my family and that is when they offered the Prescott church to me with the mess that was here. My wife was tired of moving and so I said, "Let's just go over and look at it." I had gotten some information about the church: practically all the people had left, there were two families that were solid, that was the Copeland's and the Allen's (who are still here). I told my wife, "If these two families will stay, I feel like we ought to come." And they agreed to stay if they got a good pastor. I remember as I topped the hill coming into town I just kind of felt like this is what we ought to do. So that is the call of God, who knows...it was strange circumstances. It wasn't like a fantastic opportunity or that I had an angelic visitation, it was mostly that I was at a point where I was flexible enough for what God wanted to do. I had Johnny Metzler booked for revival and I told him, "I don't know where I'll be but I want that date kept." As soon as I got here I called him. The dates were in February and I had just come in January. We had a blow out revival; of course the church only seated seventy-two people to put it in context. Our first outreach that we did in the concert scene was up in the boys club and there weren't over two-hundred if that many, but these were raw, unsaved, rebellious teenage kids. The only teenagers I'd ever seen were church kids that would rip off any convert that would come or would want to come. They would stand there and mock you and sit in the church and make remarks. When I saw these kids it looked like we were reaching the whole world. I'd never seen that many people in the church scene.

And so when you say to a pioneer pastor don't build your church on religious people you say that by experience?

W. Mitchell: Absolutely! And continued experience! Because what religious people will do is when they find a new church starting they know that they need people. So, they show up wanting an expression in music or perhaps they are rebels who have caused troubles in other churches and they show up wanting ministry. They drop money in the plate so the pastor thinks they are great, but they got problems. What they will do is establish relationship with the new converts then begin to question why you don't allow women preachers, why you put some kind of standard, or whatever. They get upset with you and they leave and pull their influence with them and take good people. That is why I say these people will hurt you because they are not your converts. A new convert will do almost anything that you would want them to do. They are like sponges; they have a heart for God. Religious people say, "They didn't believe that back in my old church so we don't have to believe that here," and they cause problems.

G. Mitchell: *"he led forth his trained men, born in his house, three hundred and eighteen...* (Gen 14:14 ASV)." *That is our pattern for building warriors.*

W. Mitchell: A guy called me one time and told me a rebel left his church and took people with him. I said, "Why does he have more influence than you have?" You have to outperform him. You have to out maneuver him. Have those people out for dinner, have them over to your house and establish relationships so that you can win these people to yourself over this rebel.

G. Mitchell: *We've seen this repeated through the years again and again. Men don't listen. Anybody who builds a church on religious people will always pay.*

W. Mitchell: We tell them over and over, "We don't want you building on religious people." Overseas this is also true, especially in third world when they see we've got a strong program and that we support our missionaries...they flock to us.

What do you look for in a city when you send a man out to pioneer?

W. Mitchell: A lot people have the idea that we've got a world map and we're pouring over this map and praying. But there are natural factors that come together; a person may have connection, relatives that are there, they may have lived there, know about the city, or they have a burden and so we work with that. The second thing is it needs to have population.

Does the size of the city matter?

W. Mitchell: It does matter; you need some population so the church could have a vision of reaching people and supporting itself. You don't start a church out on the farm. You are most successful in cities that are growing. Historically, people are most responsive when they have shifted into an area and they don't have roots there. This is in everything, not only religion but it's also in every other factor. Your hardest places to establish a new work is in your old eastern cities that are set in their ways. That is why they have such problems in the east coast in the old stable cities. The most productive areas are in the west where they are growing. People are coming in and they are the most responsive. The city ought to have some kind of financial base. Some of the cities we planted a church in the beginning I would not plant today because these dynamics are just not there. You want some kind of a stable financial base like manufacturing or something so people can get jobs. When these hippies all started to get saved here you could hardly buy a job in Prescott and all these guys had long hair. Locals used to catch hippies in the plaza and cut their hair…they didn't like hippies. One of our converts finally bought a short hair wig so he could get a job. You want some life in the city. The best is a growing city but that wouldn't be absolute because the other factors of connections can make it work.

G. Mitchell: *Historically, our strongest churches have been Hispanic based because they are very responsive to the gospel and have strong family ties. Military is another responsive group partly because of being uprooted and disconnected in the community. So those would be factors that you would look at: growth, Hispanics, military, and economy are just factors you'd look at on the surface, but that doesn't disqualify a city if there is a genuine burden that bears witness.*

God puts desires into men that are different. There are some that hate big cities and some absolutely love them. But if you are just looking…we have guys sometimes who have no burden, they don't know where to go, so it's a matter of looking at some logical factors. When I went to pioneer in Australia, everyone who had gone out before me had some kind of connection to where they were going. I had never been anywhere, so I had to choose. How do I choose? I applied logic. I thought to myself that I didn't want a town smaller than fifty-thousand because of the numbers factor. At that time I thought a city of millions would be beyond me so I decided I was looking for something between fifty and five-hundred thousand. That left only three options at that time in Australia. So using logic I decided one morning that Launceston was the place. At lunch that day somebody tells me, "I am praying for Launceston, Tasmania." Here was a city that I had never heard of until the day before looking at an atlas and now God super naturally confirms my decision.

W. Mitchell: We try to work with burden, but common sense as well. Inevitably you will have an inexperienced kid who has been raised in cow towns announce he has a burden for New York City. It's just not going to happen in his first try. This is because of the finance factor. Generally, it takes time for a man to develop; meanwhile you are investing thousands of dollars. So this is why we don't send people overseas who have never been a pastor before, because they are just trying to develop people skills, develop their preaching, and trying to learn how to be a pastor.

How does or what does the pastor's wife need to develop in the mother church before she goes and pioneers with her husband?

W. Mitchell: For one thing, just be willing to follow her husband and work with whatever she has. I'll give you an example: I had a guy called me who was pioneering and he says, "My wife is not following up on these people, and she's not doing the monthly report sheet." He had a few more complaints as well. So I said,

"Who did I send out there to pioneer?" He answered, "Well, me." Then I said, "Well then why are you putting all this on your wife?" Of course, women have abilities and that is fine, but she is called to be your wife. When there is a dominant pastor's wife, that church will have problems. So you are looking for a guy who is the head of the house. When I was in my first church we had no musicians, so my poor wife was trying to play the piano. She was practicing two or three songs every Saturday and my life was a living hell because she's not a musician. Finally I said, "This is not working; forget it and we'll do a cappella." I tried to get her to teach Sunday school and the same thing. She's trying to get this thing together and it's not her nature. So again, it's a living hell. At one time or another she has done the books. Again, I'm a detailed person and I want to know, "How much money do we have in the bank?" Well she's cooking, raising the kids, and so on and that is not her thing. She says, "I don't know." So I ask, "When are you going to know?" It just did not work so I said, "Forget about it; you raise the kids and I'll pastor." She has followed me all over the world very successfully. She's a very good wife: she's worked in the nursery, been an example as a mother, and in counseling. She's a very successful pastor's wife. I have seen the reverse where the wife is the dominant driving force and it causes major problems. We had problems in one church: one of the council members called me and said, "We need help here because anytime there is any problem or counseling the pastor must have his wife there and she's actually the one that sets the pace." When I talked to the pastor he said, "My wife has her opinions." I'm sure she did but in essence she was really the pastor and that is not what we are trying to produce. The wife may have various ministries, varying influences, but when they are very strong and dominating you are going to have problems in the congregation.

G. Mitchell: *You are looking for a disciple with a friendly and flexible wife. We have good men from time to time that you*

147

want to work with but the problem is the wife is contentious;
she's constantly fighting and that is not going to work. The
second thing is flexibility. When the wife has to have the house
a certain way, when people come in they have to have their
shoes off, etc.; that's not going to work in pioneering. Those are
trouble signs. So the woman needs to be flexible, friendly, and
have good relationships; she doesn't have to worry about the
factors of Bible study and counseling.

Is there a calling associated with being a pastor's wife?

W. Mitchell: It is really a desire to be in ministry and there is nothing wrong with that. Then you have women who feel that they are called to be preachers and they are just looking for a man to marry so they can fulfill it.

G. Mitchell: It is a desire, not necessarily a calling; if the man is not into it, then what? Then your marriage is going to be hell.

What advice would you give to a pastor of a small church?

W. Mitchell: Well, he needs to not accept the idea that he is called to be a small church pastor. The vision needs to be reaching people beyond.

Are some men called to pioneer and others called to take over churches?

W. Mitchell: Well I don't know about a calling, but some are gifted pioneering more than others. People are different.

G. Mitchell: We have men that we plant who we know from working with him he's a bit rough around the edges and lacks people skills; he would be a disaster to take an established congregation. Let him pioneer and face the reality of having no people to soften edges and later on he can take a church. On the other hand, you have the confidence factor. There are men who the thought of starting from nothing is overwhelmingly intimidating. But let them take over a work with some people that are already praying...they could work with that. I don't think that is so much a calling, nor is it written in heaven you are only called to pioneer or you are only called to take over churches. It is confidence, skill, and other things we try to work with.

Is the fear of struggle why some men don't want to pioneer?

G. Mitchell: *This comes back to the confidence factor. I still deal with guys, whether it's in this church or preaching around, who are wrestling with calling. I have talked with guys who have been saved thirty years and still don't know if they are called. I don't believe that. I believe that you are afraid or I believe that you are unwilling to put your pride on the line. I don't believe that God has lost his voice for thirty years and he just somehow can't get the message to you. Yes, there are guys who are afraid of struggle. On the other hand, you have other personalities like me who view pioneering as the most exciting thing in the entire world. To start from nothing, that's exhilarating to me. That doesn't make the men whose personality is not that invalid. In our fellowship we have leaders who have never pioneered and that is acceptable.*

It seems like many pioneer churches get stuck around thirty people. Is there any reason for that?

G. Mitchell: *People skills, people skills, and people skills. This is the guy who says, "We have only thirty, but they are commandos, they are absolute Green Beret; you know, delta force for Jesus."*

W. Mitchell: Once at a pioneer rally, this guy who had been opened five weeks testified, "I got these three guys saved, I took them out for some wings and I told them that if they were going to be Christians they were going to have to die. The next day one of them called me and said, 'I can't do it, pastor, I can't die like you told us.' So I told him, 'That's ok, we don't need any wimps.'" You aren't going to build a church that way. Guys call me about being stuck at fifty people. I ask them, "Do you have a Sunday School class?" The answer is no, so I ask, "When are you going to start one? There are people who want a Bible study. Have you got a nursery?" So, you have these factors, plus the building is too small or hidden. Sometimes it can be the pastor and his family. I remember some years ago this guy was stuck around forty people and he and his wife came for counseling. They seemed like a nice couple and everything seemed to be in order, but in the conversation the problem surfaced. After every service they would go home and analyze who was there and criticize the folks God was giving them. So through unbelief they were destroying the very thing that God wanted to do because building a church is actually a faith enterprise. You get converts who are imperfect and the pastor's job is to challenge them and cause them to be something that they are not. Another factor has to do with the home. A couple can look great, but behind the scenes the marriage is not together. It's not visible at all, but that somehow plays into the spiritual dynamic. You can be the greatest preacher in the world, but if there is something wrong back inside the home it will have an effect. That is why Paul says, *"ruling his own house well* (1 Tim 3:4 MKJV)."

G. Mitchell: *If you are talking about the fifty-range, you are probably talking about preaching skills. The man can't feed them beyond that.*

W. Mitchell: If nothing is in the well then nothing comes up in the bucket. You constantly have to be reading and observing if you are a preacher. It's a total calling, which means your whole life is dedicated to it. How do I get truth? How can I bring truth to these people? How do I make it relevant? You absolutely must develop knowledge. Through that knowledge God reveals himself and you are able to put truth into a comprehensive framework so you can communicate that. This brings us to another factor: at a certain point you are going to have to cut loose your secular employment and give yourself to your ministry. A lot of men will not live at a substandard level because of either the wife's financial decisions or the wife's demands. You can't eat out five times a week, drive the latest model car, make unwise decisions and be in debt to the point you have to work all the time. That is a major factor of why men pastor small churches. They are unwilling to discipline themselves and make the sacrifice necessary to develop. They are consumed with making a living and meeting the material needs. I'm not being hard hearted and saying I don't want them to have anything in life; it is about priorities. You are not called to a materialistic lifestyle; you are called to preach the gospel. Unless you are totally willing to give your life to that you will not develop. Generally, it will take several years to develop. You are not just going to start out with a hundred people so you can immediately quit your job. I drove ten year old cars and disciplined myself financially. My wife adjusted to fit our budget. We didn't live on credit cards and we ate basic foods like spam, stew, and a lot of spaghetti. My wife is very frugal, able to adapt, and we raised five children. She sewed a lot of clothes for the girls. So I think that is a major factor in a small church: they will build to a place that the church can support itself, and they are content to work and support their family. At some point you have to make the decision to sacrifice, downsize, and take either reduced employment or go full time as a pastor. I've known guys that have responded to this challenge and six months later they go back to work because the money is better. You are not going to do it for six months and suddenly the church grows to a hundred-fifty people. I'd say that is the major problem of why we have a lot of small churches. A little cliché that I heard in the denominational world, "The reason we have so many small churches is because we have so many small men."

Are there any things that can help to encourage a pastor when he feels discouraged? It seems that in the process of building something for God, people hit barriers and battle with discouragement.

W. Mitchell: Basically, you have to lay a hold of God. He has a solution, an answer, and a direction. This is why we have the structure we do. I just came from a pioneer rally last night and the reason we started those was to expose pioneer churches to a leadership dimension of ministry that they are not going to get locally because the church is small, isolated, and they don't get to go to conferences. A second reason was to be able to minister to pastors. I limit my preaching schedule to where I can touch primarily pastors. That is what I spend most of my life doing. I want to impart to them a spirit, a pattern of preaching that makes sense that they can tie on to bring help, and a pattern for their own ministry. A lot of these young pastors need development. We try to spend our time in formats where we can help these young pastors. I'm going to Las Vegas to preach and do a crusade and we are going to have three or four pastors in a group and we'll put together a sermon; it is crucial to teach these young pastors how to make a sermon.

G. Mitchell: Discouragement is a failure of the will. Therefore, encouragement must come from within. You have to lay hold of God. The Bible says, "David encouraged himself in the LORD his God (1 Sam 30:6 KJV)." Another factor is relationship; you have to stay connected to brethren. The third thing is commitment to obedience regardless of feelings. If you can only function when you feel good then you won't function. That is why the Bible says, "act like men (1 Corinthians 16:13 ESV)." In the garden Jesus prayed, "not my will, but yours be done (Luke 22:42 ESV)." There is a commitment of the will to obedience that releases encouragement.

W. Mitchell: There was a great temptation for me to give up after the split in ninety, but God dealt with me to keep doing what he had called me to do and he would take care of me. You can't give up just because you have been burned or things are not going right. People ask, "How do you keep going?" My standard answer is, "I have a relationship with Jesus." Over and above all, you have to have that personal relationship with the Lord. Regardless of what happens in life, he is the one you are to obey and do what he has called you to do. It is not all about you. The Kingdom is about Him. You have to look at the larger picture. In Psalms 73, the author was ready to backslide, but then he went into the house of God and gained perspective.

What would be the essentials in a building?

W. Mitchell: Location is important. You don't want to be in a horrible area where nobody wants to go. Do not start a church in the ghetto. You need to build in a blue-collar neighborhood and build out of blue-collar people. You will spin in some of these welfare folks and the health of the congregation will bring help to them to break out of that. The Bible says, "And the common people heard him gladly (Mark 12:37 KJV)." That is what we reach for.

G. Mitchell: *It will increase your chances of gathering people instead of limiting. Our churches are historically middle class to lower middle class. That is what we typically build on. We have a few upper-middle class and wealthy people that come in and we certainly reach into poverty areas but middle-class is what we reach and what makes sense for what we do.*

W. Mitchell: Also, it's important that you pick up papers and garbage so it doesn't seem trashy. You would be astonished how many pastors couldn't care less about that. You have to watch out for zoning; it's best to sign a month to month lease if you can so you make sure if you get shut down you can break that lease. Some guys can function for years without ever getting an occupancy permit; other guys get a red tag the minute he hangs the sign. Every city is different. In areas like Los Angeles, to apply for an occupancy permit it cost ten-thousand dollars...just to apply. And they know they are not going to give it to you because they don't want churches there. Cities don't want churches in buildings because of the tax base; they want businesses in there.

How successful have we been opening up in hotels?

W. Mitchell: I wouldn't say it's largely successful but it's better than nothing. I say again, we encourage you to open a Bible study in your house, witness in your apartment complex or neighborhood and get some people saved. Don't wait for the big banner opening. As soon as you can you need a building so you can put a nursery because young families are most responsive to our ministry and you want to get the screaming kids out of the main auditorium. You ought to have twelve to fifteen hundred square feet.

G. Mitchell: *Visibility, distance, danger, and socio-economic factors all play into a building.*

Is there a guideline for how soon a pioneer church should be a certain size?

G. Mitchell: *No because it's just numbers and the devil doesn't cooperate.*

W. Mitchell: After eighteen months we have the option to bring you back for redirection with a good attitude to help us here in the mother church.

G. Mitchell: *But that is simply a guideline. That is purely dependant on the man and there are many factors. We don't want guys going screwy because long-term bareness does bad things to men. So it isn't automatic that we bring men back after eighteen months; it simply gives us a guideline. It motivates a man to know we will not allow him to be there forever. If he's comfortable financially he's not motivated. Some men will have ten people for ten years and six are his family. How can you do that? He could be doing more good in the mother church. So it gives us a guideline but that depends on the man. If he doesn't keep contact that is a bad sign and we are probably going to start at eighteen months to pressure him because he is lost in space.*

W. Mitchell: And then you have to understand this is our guideline for Prescott. Every church planter has his own preference. Sometimes we leave a man in a place simply because we do not have a replacement.

G. Mitchell: *It's not meant to be an across the board rule but it is more of a recognition that you cannot let a man stay forever without progress...it's unhealthy in every way.*

W. Mitchell: He starts to reason that church planting doesn't work, he's been wronged, or this is my calling. I had one guy that told me his ministry was to fertilize (not reap).

G. Mitchell: I had a man ask me once in all sincerity, "Do you believe that God sends some men to cities simply as a witness to judge that city." Of course, the man who asked this had a small church. Because of long-term barrenness he created his own theology. In Australia, when I was pioneering, I rebelled against this. We had a number of struggling pastors and what we heard over and over again in their preaching was all the scriptures to justify why you can't believe for anything. I reject that! It doesn't line up with the Bible.

W. Mitchell: Encouraging faith and making right some of these mentalities is another reason for having pioneer rallies. Pioneering is a faith proposition.

Is there a guideline for when a man should quit his job and go full time in the ministry? Is it a number like sixty people or is it more to do with church income?

W. Mitchell: It depends on the demographics of a city and what the economy there is like. Some places are extremely expensive and you will need a sizeable group before you can have enough income to go full time. But the answer to the question is as soon as possible. You have to encourage the worker to have that as a goal. You will never build a church without sacrifice. We don't send men out to die but the person must be willing to make a sacrifice and that will generally mean downsizing their standard of living. We ask guys what kind of debt they have before sending them out. So, if they are making car payments on a new car, five-hundred-eighty a month, and thousands in credit card debt then you disqualify yourself.

How soon should a pioneer pastor preach on money?

G. Mitchell: I would say in the first year you do preach on money. It might be instruction before the offering, Bible study, or perhaps a sermon, but the emphasis should be on the blessings of obedience. In other words, in a brand new work you do not preach, "Will a man rob God?" or "You are going to burn in hell if you don't tithe!" Generally speaking, you should tell stories about God's provision that challenge and stir faith. That being said, often when a man is moving toward being self-supporting and he preaches on money he will feel a resistance and therefore he backs off. That man will never break through. It is more than raising money. I remember very clearly as a disciple in Perth, dad preached on money in the morning and felt a resistance. So, he preached that night on money again. Of course, that was not a pioneer church; he was trying to break a stronghold. I've seen him press in during altar calls when he feels resistance.

W. Mitchell: When we preach on money we give altar calls. We preach for a verdict. The first revival I had in Prescott was with John Metzler and he preached on money every night and took an offering besides the regular offering already received. I attribute the break through that we experienced and the dimensions established in this church right at the beginning to that revival.

How important is establishing praise in the pioneer church?

W. Mitchell: Al Fury told the story in one revival that he had sixteen people and he was trying to get them to praise God. He said he told the congregation that if they were not going to praise God they needed to find another church. The next service there was nobody. So he said he has learned that sixteen people not praising God is better than zero people all praising God. There is sensitivity, orchestration, and timing to all of life. It does need to be contended for. There are some things we must contend for or you won't have them. Prayer, giving, and praise all must be contended for and you will be resisted. Also, you must give biblical basis. A lot of guys want people to do things but never give biblical reasons.

G. Mitchell: Balance is the key. It is important for the pastor and his wife to establish praise. It is important to preach on praise. But on the other hand, I've seen guys who have three people and they praise God for ten minutes straight at the top of their lungs in a neo-Nazi frenzy, banging the pulpit, "You sound like dead religious people."

W. Mitchell: The first way you contend is to be an example. You are not going to get people to pray if you don't pray; same with praise and giving. In our church you will see the staff contributing during offering. I've been to places where they never pass the plate on the platform because there is nobody there that gives. Something is wrong there. You need to set the example. No matter where I go or how late I get back I'm in prayer the next morning. In Perth, I would often land at three a.m. and I would be in prayer meeting that morning. It is very important. People need to know that the staff prays.

Are there any concluding thoughts?

G. Mitchell: These are the three largest factors that I see: one is faith, I have never seen a man who is busting out in revival who is filled with unbelief. A man who has faith will never tell you how many demons per square inch are in his city; he believes God. I have seen over and over again men who come up with reasons why they can't have revival in their city and it is simply their unbelief. Secondly, people skills are a major factor and we talked about that. The third thing is what I call dominion. Pastor Mitchell called it earlier a supernatural dimension. There is an element of pioneering that is warfare. Workers will call and say, "Pastor, every time I get someone saved a religious person comes and grabs them (or something else steals the convert)." There has to be something in a man that rises up and says, "This is from hell." He has to touch God and get a breakthrough; fight the enemy off the well and therefore establish dominion. Pioneering is very much linked in with dominion. Now the problem is how to do that? I cannot quantify it: if you pray this much, read this much, and do this you will have dominion. I can tell you what I've done and what I've seen other men do, but most of it is a spirit that says, "I am not going to let the devil win and rip these people off." One of the all time classic stories is Mark Aulson coming to Pastor Mitchell and saying, "I witness to people all the time and I can't get anybody saved." So dad told him to fast. Mark went on a three day fast and nothing changed. When he came back to pastor to complain he was told to fast again. And so he fasted again. At the end of that three day fast he went to work and a lady came to him (Sue Rush) to inquire about salvation and he prayed with her. She then brought her boyfriend and several others who got saved that are all in the church to this day. That is an example of dominion being established. Mark touched God. Now that does not mean that the key is doing back to back three-day fasts and you will have dominion. You will hear Pastor Mitchell say all the time to pioneers, "You better find out where God is!" So, there is a threefold cord: you will never break through if you don't believe god. If you don't have people skills you will run off everybody God brings. And the third is the supernatural dimension or dominion where you determine the spiritual factors instead of the devil.

W. Mitchell: There is no doubt that we are unique. We have partnered together to reach the world and there is a real gratitude and appreciation for the mother church. We help each other without being afraid that another church is going to proselyte our best musician and lead disciple. There is an ethics that is embedded into our mentalities. There are built into our fellowship a lot of reference points that sometimes can be taken for granted. For instance, in our fellowship we see people get saved. People do not realize how rare that is. We see people get healed. I remember when I was in Bible school I had a divine healing class at Angeles Temple where the whole Foursquare movement began out of the healing ministry of Aimee Simple McPherson. As the professor is talking about miracles of healing, this old guy walking down the hall overhears, sticks his head in the door and says, "Yea, but we don't believe that anymore." It is now just a doctrine there. So, we see people healed, saved, and transformed. It is such a reference point for people saved in this fellowship. The religious world doesn't see this.

G. Mitchell: Last night we had one of the disciples do a neighborhood outreach. He called it a block party, invited the neighbors out and had food and music. There were seventy-five visitors. He preached and had an altar call and had thirteen people saved. There are pastors in the religious world who have never seen seventy-five visitors in their entire ministry.

W. Mitchell: The number of people saved is in direct proportion to the number of people who are confronted with the gospel. The basic premise of evangelism is get outside of the four walls of the church building.

G. Mitchell: Men can say they are called all they want, but are they involved in evangelism? This guy who did the outreach, he and his wife, have committed themselves to working with people. They are experiencing pioneering on a small scale. They are growing and learning real life people skills. You cannot get that in a class room. Being involved in ministry is a key in discipleship. This is why I love the weekly concert ministry; it is a training ground for pioneering. The concert ministry director will come to me and say, "We have had no visitors or people saved two weeks in a row." So I respond, "Okay, what are you going to do about that? If you were pioneering and nobody was getting saved what would you do about it?" So, they rise up between themselves and call a fast, extra outreach, or whatever. Every concert director will come to me at some point and say, "The people are not praying enough, etc." I ask, "What do you want to do about it?" Typically, they say they want to call a meeting and lay down the law. I laugh and explain to them how in a forty year old church you will have people who will listen politely for two seconds and then tune you out. Others will work against you out of spite and you will have nothing but hell from now on. Perhaps a couple of the newer people will listen and work with you. Instead of giving orders, why don't you get along side these people and tell them you need them. It is called taking ownership. Say to them, "Have you noticed that prayer has been lacking? What can we do about that? I need your help; what can you do to help me?" This is a people skill and a pastoral skill. A concert director will come and say, "There are visitors and I think I should pull the altar call now." So he is becoming sensitive, he is learning. I will not make the choice for him. When they do it and it works there is something put in them. We had a concert one night where a bunch of visitors *came in right after the altar call. So the director told me, "I think we should have the bands play some more." He did that and at the second altar call another six people were saved. So those are the things that involvement in ministry reveals: does a man have sensitivity, a concern, can he humble himself when he wants to burn everybody, and will he learn these things or not. That is the beauty of discipleship. Things get flushed out.*

Closing remark?

W. Mitchell: It really does help if you like people. It really helps if the pastor's wife likes people. We are in the people business and if you don't like people it is not going to work.

About the Author

David J. Drum has over twenty years of ministry experience with the Christian Fellowship Ministries; serving as pastor, international evangelist and missionary for five years in Soweto, South Africa. David resides with his wife Hilda in El Paso, TX.

For more information visit: www.davidjdrum.com

Acknowledgements

It was Matt McDonald who first gave me the idea of doing this book and I appreciate his encouragement along the way. I would like to thank Pastor Mitchell for the opportunity and Greg Mitchell for proof reading the text.

Gratitude to my wonderful wife Hilda for patience and support during this project; she transcribed the vast majority of the sermons for the book.

Gracias to Ed Kidwell at Kidwell Publishing for walking me through the whole editing and publishing process; to Luke Gallegos for cover design; also I would like to thank all those who read and re-read portions of the book while it was in its infant stages.

Other titles from Kidwell Publishing available through your favorite bookstore or online at: www.kidwellpublishing.com

Twice Dead: The True Death and Life Story of Roman Gutierrez
By David J. Drum
ISBN: 978-0-9856041-0-3
When Roman Gutierrez was eleven years old, his father died from a heroin overdose. Roman resolved, in his anger and his pain, that someday God would take him the same way. He became an addict, a year later he went to juvenile detention for stealing, and attempted suicide the year after that. At fifteen he got into a fight and was pronounced dead for six minutes. At nineteen he was stabbed by his best friend, and pronounced dead for five minutes. When Roman was twenty-five, he shot up all the heroin he had so his torment would end ... and realized he didn't want to die. That's when a miracle occurred...

Muerto Dos Veces ("Twice Dead" in Spanish)
By David J. Drum
ISBN: 978-0-9817634-6-0
Cuando Román Gutiérrez tenía once años, su padre murió por una sobredosis de heroína. Román ha resuelto, en su ira y su dolor, que algún día Dios se lo llevará de la misma manera. Se convirtió en un adicto, un año más tarde se fue a la detención de menores por robar, e intento de suicidio al año siguiente. A los quince años se metió en una pelea y fue declarado muerto por seis minutos. A los diecinueve años que fue apuñalado por su mejor amigo, y declarado muerto durante cinco minutos. Cuando Román tenía veinticinco, se injectó toda la heroína que tenía para que su tormento se acabaría ... y se dió cuenta que no quería morir. Fué entonces cuando ocurrió un milagro ...

Spiritual Power: How To Get It, How To Give It
By Don W. Basham
ISBN: 978-0-9817634-8-4
With over 125,000 copies in print, this book has been the authoritative guide on the topic of the baptism in the Holy Spirit with the evidence of speaking in tongues for approximately four decades. Author Don W. Basham neither denies nor ignores any of the controversy surrounding speaking in tongues. Instead, he provides a firm scriptural basis for those who might have questions or doubts about tongues, and encourages anyone interested how they can personally experience the blessing God offers through the baptism in the Holy Spirit with the confirming evidence of speaking in tongues.

(Continued on next page)

Offering Stories, Quotes, and Illustrations
Volume 1
By Robert Polaco
ISBN: 978-0-9817634-5-3
Volume 1 is a compilation of over 200 offering stories, quotes, and illustrations. Each illustration also contains a note line where pastors or administrators can indicate the date on which the illustration was used, preventing the potential embarrassment of reusing an illustration. This is a must have companion for any pastor or church administrator.

Offering Stories, Quotes, and Illustrations
Volume 2
By Robert Polaco
ISBN: 978-0-9817634-7-7
Volume 2 is the anticipated sequel in Robert Polaco's compilation series, and includes 375 new entries organized with descriptive titles. This is a must have companion for any pastor or church administrator, filled with illustrations that inspire people to liberality. These illustrations often include supporting scriptural references, and each entry includes a line where one can choose to write in where or when it was used.

The Pilgrim's Progress – Part I and Part II
By John Bunyan
ISBN: 978-0-9817634-3-9
This timeless class of John Bunyan "delivered under the similtude of a dream" captures the hearts and minds of readers with Bunyan's depth of understanding and scriptural knowledge, as well as his subtle comedy and witticisms.
This edition contains both parts of Bunyan's tale, including all of the original scripture references in an easy-to-read format.

Freedom To Choose
By E. L. Kidwell
ISBN: 978-0-9817634-1-5
Visit the Kingdom of Heaven before Earth was created. Enter the throne room of God, and experience the events before time began. Discover the secrets of why hell's chief accuser betrayed the love and perfection of His Creator, and set himself to destroy the race of mankind in seething hatred. Enjoy this thought-provoking drama as it brings to life the Genesis account of the Bible.

CPSIA information can be obtained
at www.ICGtesting.com
Printed in the USA
BVHW071625090819
555520BV00002B/177/P